THE FRENCH REVOLUTION

One of the most critical events in modern history, the French Revolution, has left later generations a wealth of authentic graphic material which dramatically recreates those momentous years—paintings, engravings, broadsheets, newspaper cartoons, prints, drawings, and other visual sources. In this volume, hundreds of the best of these have been carefully selected and edited, to present a detailed view of origins, course, and results for the immediate future of France.

The first sections examine the mainsprings of revolution in the *ancien régime*, and distinguish the elements of crisis which confronted French government and society in 1789. In discussing the complex chain of events which followed, one particular aspect emerges—the power of the Paris mob. It was this which gave the French Revolution its characteristic atmosphere of violence and confusion, a state of affairs which virtually no amount of political jobbery or idealism could check. In this context, Professor Johnson illustrates Louis XVI's relations with the assemblies, his abortive flight to Varennes in June, 1791, and his trial and execution. He illustrates the various roles played by Robespierre, Danton, Mirabeau, Bailly, Lafayette and others in a deteriorating situation, dominated by the National Guard, and by the *sans-culottes* and *enragés*. Other sections examine France's involvement in European war, and the republican army, before and after Robespierre's death, and the Thermidorian Reaction of 1794. The final sections look at France under the Directory, and analyze the events which led up to Napoleon Bonaparte's bid for power.

THE WAYLAND PICTORIAL SOURCES SERIES

THE FRENCH REVOLUTION

DOUGLAS JOHNSON

WAYLAND PUBLISHERS LONDON

The Wayland Pictorial Sources Series

The Medieval Establishment   GEOFFREY HINDLEY
The Voyages of Discovery   G. R. CRONE & ALAN KENDALL
The American Revolution   ROGER PARKINSON
Shakespeare's England   LEVI FOX
The Dawn of Man   VINCENT MEGAW & RHYS JONES
The Russian Revolution   LIONEL KOCHAN
The American Civil War   KEITH ELLIS
Twentieth Century China   JOHN ROBOTTOM
Medieval Warfare   GEOFFREY HINDLEY

Picture research by the Publishers

Copyright © 1970 by Wayland (Publishers) Ltd
101 Grays Inn Road London WC1
SBN 85340 025 3

Printed in Great Britain by Jarrold and Sons Ltd, Norwich

CONTENTS

CHAPTER ONE
THE SEEDS OF REVOLUTION

THE POET T. S. ELIOT once remarked that we could probably never be right about someone as great as Shakespeare; but it mattered that, from time to time, we should change our way of being wrong. The same can be said about the French Revolution of 1789; historians have constantly modified their way of looking at it.

Sometimes, the Revolution has been seen as a conspiracy, a catastrophe caused by small, identifiable, groups of men, such as freemasons, or British agents. Others have seen it as the result of the European Enlightenment, represented by the so-called *philosophes* of the eighteenth century, with their restlessness and desire for change. Or was the Revolution an accident of history, a chain of haphazard events, affected by the weakness of Louis XVI and the political folly of his Queen, Marie-Antoinette?

The French Revolution has also been set on a grander stage, by historians who believed that the people made a conscious revolt against feudalism and injustice. They point to the middle classes, conscious of their economic importance, who aimed at political and social advancement. They point to the lower classes, aware of their poverty and alarmed for their well-being; and they see the peasantry as concerned for their lands and resentful of exactions by aristocracy and Church alike. One can hold a similar view of French history, but place responsibility for the Revolution instead on a different class, the privileged

aristocracy. According to this school of thought, it was the aristocracy who first flouted royal authority, especially in provincial districts, and thereby launched the crisis. Picture (1) shows aristocrats in the time of Louis XIV.

But behind these social movements lay other factors, to which many historians have attached great significance: the financial crisis of the government, for example, worsened by participation in the American War of Independence. The economic depression, which coincided roughly with Louis XVI's reign, interrupted the long period of rising prices, which had enriched all the producing classes. The bad harvest of 1788, too, brought about a spectacular rise in the price of bread, then the staple food commodity. Modern writers have taken a special interest in the factor of collective action. They have noted the panic in the countryside, the fear of brigands and whisperings of aristocratic plots. They have rejected superficial mentions of "crowds" and "mobs," and have tried to understand both the psychology and the procedure of mass actions. Sometimes, they have seen these happenings as the work of individual activists. So the idea of conspiracy comes full circle.

Most of these writers have stressed the importance of the Revolution, not only for the history of France and the world, but because it was the blueprint of revolution in modern society. It had its alternating periods of moderation and violence, its high ideals and bitterness, its dominating fears and clinging hopes. The French Revolution, more than any revolution has done before or since, created personalities who climbed into strongholds of power, only to be cast aside by events. This was a period of violent energy, and at the same time, fatigue. It can be argued, as well, that the way in which the Revolution came to be dominated by war, and eventually by a soldier (Napoleon), also typifies many revolutions.

Yet, the Revolution has also been played down. Some historians have always asked: what did the Revolution really accomplish? If its achievement was to consolidate a landowning peasantry and a centralized system of administration, then surely these were already features of pre-Revolutionary France? The Revolution did not create, it only affirmed. One should stress the continuity of French history, rather than the Revolution as the promoter of great changes. Historians who adopt this viewpoint often display more objectivity than those who claim the Revolution as a step forward for humanity, or as the threshold of a period of decadence for the French people.

Historians, therefore, have adopted many different standpoints. They have followed fashions, they have changed their minds. Sometimes the change has followed the discovery of new source material; sometimes it has come from asking different questions. But one problem remains in the forefront of debate: why did the Revolution take place at the end of the eighteenth century? After all, this century had not been a bad one for France as a whole. The population had risen from about twenty to twenty-six millions; no great plagues or other catastrophes had occurred; no wars had been fought on French soil; industry had thrived; the general rise of prices from about 1730 to the eve of the Revolution was a sign of the prosperity of the producing classes; overseas trade multiplied. The Bourbon monarchy was the first monarchy of Europe, and no signs of disloyalty to it could be detected in France. This picture of a prosperous nation—contrasting, for example, with the last years of Louis XIV —has led historians to explain the Revolution in terms of conspiracy or accident.

But in reality, there were many crises. The phenomenon of 1789 is that they all came alive and reached a climax at around the same time. The most obvious one was social: if general prosperity existed, it was unequally distributed. Vast sections of the

1

French people suffered from the rise of prices, rather than profited from it. Although the peasantry, for example, owned their land, they often farmed such a small acreage that they had no food to sell on the open market. The expanding town populations, and those who formed a "rural proletariat," were the losers, since wages lagged behind prices. Prosperity came only to those who held fairly large estates, who exercised feudal rights, or who could manipulate farm rents. The mass of peasant producers resented this class, in both a rational and emotional way. Their resentment was shared by a distant social class—the urban bourgeoisie.

It is hard to generalize about such an amorphous, varied class as the bourgeoisie, yet one can say that during the eighteenth century they were growing in numbers and wealth. But they still found themselves barred from innumerable state posts, because they lacked aristocratic birth. Growing more self-confident, more self-conscious, they became impatient with the lax and irrational methods by which France was ruled. Like the peasantry, they found it simple to blame the aristocracy for this. Their hostility was easily extended towards the Church: here, they said, was privilege and superstition locking up the wealth of the country in a totally unprofitable way. What was the attitude of the aristocracy? A small class of varying wealth, they stressed their separation from other classes by insisting, more than ever,

on their exclusive privileges, and by raising rents on their estates wherever possible. All these strains had the making of a crisis; few people could have guessed how extensive it would be.

There was also an administrative crisis. The French constitution was hard to define; the authority of the king was, in theory, boundless and all-pervading, and was exercised by royal officials—intendants—in the provinces. But rights and privileges also belonged to the Estates (provincial assemblies), to the Parlements (law-courts), and to those towns which held charters. The aristocracy and the Church had privileges in taxation and in the courts. Thus, a great many different forces had to be accommodated in the running of the country. The worse the financial crisis became, the harder this task became too, and the greater the need for reform.

Higher government spending during the eighteenth century was a part of the general price rise; it was also a sign of growing governmental activity. Like governments elsewhere, that of the French was forced into greater debt, until the annual interest payments became formidable. Income was easily overtaken by expenditure. This situation could never be remedied without bringing all the social and administrative difficulties out into the open.

In any case, remedies were made more difficult by the economic slump and fall of prices in the 1780s. Everyone concerned with production, including the land-owners, was hit. They became even more determined not to yield any privileges. The government could find no way to raise funds. How could the country find its way out of the crisis?

France was not alone in facing such problems. Other countries knew similar crises during the eighteenth century. It has been suggested that certain nations with Atlantic shores ought to be considered together, since each had similar difficulties. But in France, the great debate about reform seemed to be the sharpest; the thought and ideas of the Enlightenment seemed to have a special effect. Possibly the French were more uncertain as to what their government could, and should, do.

The French Revolution perhaps appears more significant than in other countries, because it forms the climax of the European Enlightenment. Then, when it became caught up in a general European war and a vital part of European history, it gained a unique and dramatic importance.

The pages which follow do not seek to tell the whole history of the French Revolution, nor is a pictorial presentation meant to replace general historical treatment. A bibliography of authoritative works which the reader should consult is given at the end. To recount the history of the French Revolution with the aid of pictures left to history by men of the time is simply a way of recreating a great event which is always in need of new examination.

A famous view of the Palace of Versailles was painted in 1668 by Pierre Patel (2). Perhaps there was never a greater symbol of the wealth and power of any European monarchy than this magnificent monument to Louis XIV, *Le Roi Soleil* (The Sun King). The château is seen here from the east; it has not yet been transformed by the architects Louis Le Vau and François Mansart. Louis XIV is shown arriving in a carriage drawn by six horses, with the Queen following in the next carriage behind.

The French state had reached a climax of achievement in the reign of Louis XIV. But this had been the result of a long process of transformation. Whether in architecture or in politics, Louis XIV had always made his plans

2

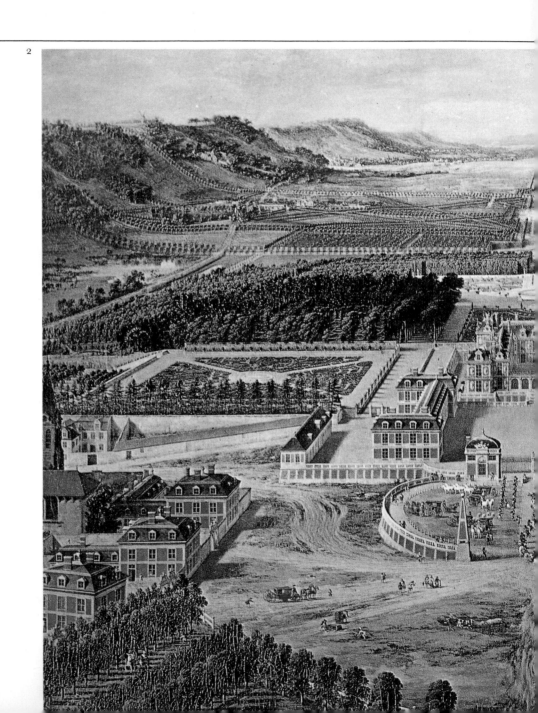

on a long-term basis. He had acted and ruled on the assumption that he would live to be old, and for a hundred years the process of change had continued.

It was always accepted that France should be ruled over by a king. It was accepted, too, that his subjects should be of different classes— those who were privileged, and those who were not. It is to these classes, and the position they occupied in the French social and political order, that we will now turn. For here we will find some of the keys to understanding the greatest crisis in French history, a crisis which came to a head in the century after Pierre Patel painted this picture. We will look first of all at the French monarchy.

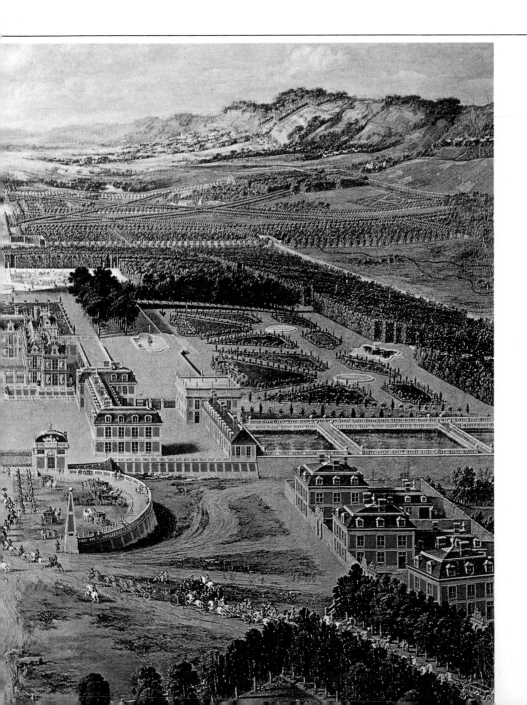

The growth of the power of the French monarchs owed a debt to its greatest ministers, such as the Cardinal de Richelieu (3) in the time of Louis XIII.

A few kilometres from Paris, Versailles was the greatest of several magnificent palaces belonging to the monarchy; the Trianon one kilometre from Versailles was another (4). The superiority of monarchy over aristocracy was demonstrated by the attendance of the nobility at court and the privilege of attending the *lever du roi* (rising of the king) at the beginning of the day. A *lever* of Louis XV held in 1722 was pictured by Pierre Dulin (5).

The entertainments staged by the court were lavish and spectacular, especially in the

3 4

5

time of Louis XV. The Palace of Versailles had its own playhouse (6), attended by the royal family and the court. Fireworks were used to celebrate great state occasions, as on the Pont-Neuf in Paris in 1745 (7).

When Louis XV was succeeded by his grandson, Louis XVI, in 1774, royal extravagance was somewhat reduced. The grandson was not as professional a spendthrift as the grandfather, and in any case, as we shall see, Louis XVI's government was crippled by financial difficulties. Louis's second brother, the Comte d'Artois, was booed by a Parisian crowd after registering royal stamp and land measures (8). The Parisians saw in this act of royal authority a threat to their own city magistrates.

6 7

8

An old cartoon shows France, represented as a globe, being supported by the people (9). The privileged orders, the nobility and the clergy, stand aside. The first order ("estate") of the kingdom was the clergy. Officially, all France is Catholic. The scepticism of French aristocrats and intellectuals has become famous, yet most French people cherish the Catholic faith. The main home of the Church in Paris in 1789 was the Cathedral of Notre-Dame (11).

The clergy numbered less than 150,000. A deep gulf separated the highest and lowest members of the hierarchy. At the humblest level, the country priest was hardly different from the peasantry. But at the top, rich and powerful families ruled through men like Cardinal Rohan, Bishop of Strasbourg. This bishop was tricked into presenting a priceless diamond necklace, as he thought, to Marie-Antoinette, and for his duplicity was upbraided

9

by Louis XVI and the Queen (10). He was condemned to the Bastille prison, but with his power and riches, he could still live in sumptuous style.

The Second Estate, the aristocracy, formed a coherent group, representing perhaps one and a half per cent of the population. There were more than 300,000 of them. As a result, not all the nobility were able to be resident at the court of Versailles. This was the privilege of the upper nobility who claimed the right by birth. But in Paris, and in other towns, the aristocracy were the leaders of fashionable life. Charles-Maurice Talleyrand, the French statesman and diplomat, once said that whoever had not lived under the *ancien régime* did not know *la douceur du vivre*. The fashions of ladies and gentlemen could be very elegant (13, 14), and the costume of the nobility, as in the time of Louis XIV, extremely elaborate (12).

12

10　11　　13　14

The most privileged businessmen were the financiers, especially the independent *fermiers généraux* (tax farmers) who contracted to raise the indirect taxes on behalf of the government. By the time of the Revolution, these men had almost become a branch of the government. They were a closed caste, nominating their own successors. Taxation was supplemented by loans on the international money market, which brought bankers even greater influence.

One of the greatest of these was the Swiss banker, Jacques Necker (19). The marriage of his daughter, Germaine, to the Swedish Ambassador in Paris, De Staël, was an affair of state. The marriage contract was signed in January, 1786, by the King and Queen of France and all the princes of the blood. Some even thought the Neckers could have done better by their daughter. The national debt allied banking interests to the government, but

19

20

21

bankers always lived in fear of repudiation of the debt.

Economic conditions in France varied from one part to another. Despite growing industrial production, the use of steampower and an organized working force, the pace and extent of industrialization was less than in England. Most town industries were still dominated by the closed guild system. Merchant manufacturers may have been frustrated by this, considering the prosperity of seaports like Bordeaux (21). A cartoon shows the merchant crushed by the weight of Church and state taxes (22). When the English writer Arthur Young visited Bordeaux in 1787, he was deeply impressed: "We must not name Liverpool in competition with Bordeaux." A sign of Bordeaux's magnificence was Victor Louis's Théâtre (20), which was built between 1770 and 1780.

20

The French merchant marine was said to have doubled in the fifty years before the Revolution, and the amount of trade grew five times in the century as a whole. Some French ports thrived by the triangular slave trade: goods from the Atlantic coast to West Africa, slaves from there to the West Indies, and sugar from the West Indies back home. Much of this sugar was, in its turn, exported. France had a profitable cod trade, too, in which the busy port of Saint-Malo was prominent (23). This commerce was approved of by contemporaries, because it took little out of the country, and trained seamen for naval service. Saint-Malo suffered many disadvantages as a port, including a difficult entry. Like Rochefort (24), and unlike Bordeaux, it lacked a prosperous hinterland. The activity of such ports contrasted with

23

24

the poverty of much of the countryside which lay behind them. They thus indicate something of the diversity of French economic and social life. Economic activity, and the work of state officials, caused many towns to grow. The small provincial capitals like Rennes, Dijon, Grenoble, remained small, with populations little more than 20,000 by the 1750s, but Marseilles and Bordeaux were both approaching 100,000. Lyons had about 160,000, and Paris more than half a million. Paris itself was a city of contrasts. It boasted the Champs-Élysées (26), an elegant tree-lined avenue created by the Marquis de Marigny, brother of Madame de Pompadour, in 1764. But, in its heart, Paris was an overcrowded maze of narrow dirty streets and cul-de-sacs. After a storm its gutters often became flooded (25).

25

26

22

The engravings reproduced on this page are part of the historian Anthony Lacroix's collection of scenes of Parisian life around the time of the French Revolution. These were the kind of people—small tradesmen, craftsmen and workers—who collectively played such a powerful role in the tumultuous years of the Revolution. Paris was full of street traders, for example: wood-seller (27), stoneware-vendor

(28), cobbler (29), barrel-maker (30), lantern merchant (31), peddlers selling novelties such as toy windmills (32), or household items like scissors, knives and combs (33), vinegar (34), and bootlaces (35). Some sold country produce, for example, the milkmaid (36), and lettuce-seller (37). Nor was entertainment lacking, as we can see from the organ-player (38), the magic lantern (39), the official an-

nouncing the lottery winners (40), and the hurdy-gurdy player (41). Other Parisians were concerned with city sanitation, for example the well-cleaner (42), sweeper (43), chimney-sweep (44), and rat-catcher (45). The bill-sticker (46), print-seller (47), *provencal*, or fife and drum player (48), and ink-seller (49), all played a part in spreading news, and probably rumours. Paris had its down-and-outs too, like this blind man with his staff (50).

Paris was a noisy and vigorous city, and Parisians of every class were proud of their citizenship and jealous of what they considered to be their rights. They would not have envied the life led by the peasantry in the provinces. France was not a great urban country; no other city could possibly rival the Parisians' claims to national leadership.

39   40   41   42

43   44   45   46

47   48   49   50

But life under the *ancien régime* was essentially the life of the peasantry (53). Three-quarters of the population lived and worked on the land, toiling at a subsistence agriculture dominated by cereal crops. Figure (51) shows a communal meal during a harvest on a provincial estate. The seigneur and his family sit apart, on the right. Grapes for wine were widely cultivated, often in soil and climatic conditions which would not be thought suitable today. What distinguished France from other European countries was the fact that a landowning peasantry, possessing between a third and a quarter of the land, coexisted with a privileged seignorial system. But few of the peasants owned enough land to support their families throughout the year; they were an impoverished section of the population (52).

52 53

bien chaud qui tout ses habits porte
néanmoins contre ces francs Narquois
moindre hiver la rigueur est trop forte
ant aux pieds que la paille et le bois

Their misery changed little over the years.

Such was the realm of the Bourbons. From 1774, the King was Louis XVI, the grandson of Louis XV. He was only twenty when he came to the throne, a kindly, well-intentioned young man, conscious of his own inadequacies. Like all the Bourbons, he was devoted to hunting; but, unusually, and a sign of the times, he had learned a craft, and had become an amateur locksmith. Joseph-Sifrède Duplessis's portrait suggests a certain dullness behind the royal splendour (55). His Queen, Marie-Antoinette (54), was the daughter of Francis I and Maria Theresa of Austria. Ever since the scandal of Cardinal Rohan's necklace in 1786, she had been disliked by the French people. She was more unhappy than frivolous, but decidedly lacked political sense.

55

54

The pressure mounted on the government to reform. For two years Anne Robert-Jacques Turgot (57) had held office as chief minister, introducing a number of reforms into the finances and the administration. When Louis XVI was persuaded to turn against Turgot and dismiss him, the demand for reform did not stop. Countless minor writers and pamphleteers reiterated the ideas of the leaders of the Enlightenment. The leading writers included Jean-Jacques Rousseau (58), known for his belief in man's goodness and for his sentimental approach to religion, rather than for his political thought. One of his most famous works was *La Nouvelle Héloïse*. François Voltaire, caricatured in figure (56), was famous for his attacks on injustice and on the Church. Although Rousseau and Voltaire held different

56

57

58

beliefs, both played a part in a general intellectual movement which demanded a rational organization of the state, and which argued about the basic human rights and nature of man.

Figure (59) is a map showing the provinces of France under the *ancien régime*. The intendant was the local instrument of royal power. He worked within a *généralité* which could itself be divided into smaller areas, for example bailiwicks and dioceses. In those areas known as the *pays d'élection* the intendants and their officers made the decisions concerning taxation. But in other parts of France, often where the old provinces had been late in joining the kingdom, there existed provincial estates which kept to themselves the right to decide how the taxes were to be paid.

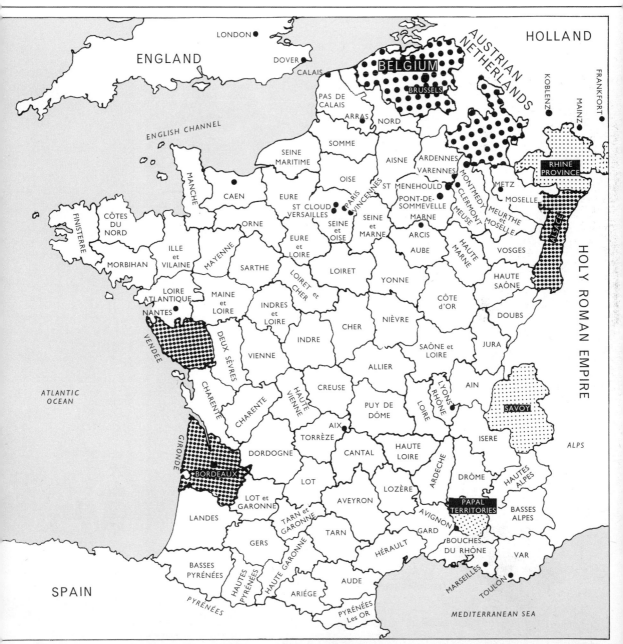

59

The first signs of crisis were financial. From 1776 to 1781 the Genevan banker, Jacques Necker, was in charge of the finances. In 1781 he presented an account to the King. He claimed that all was well: that his policy of financing by borrowing was successful. But within a short time, no more money could be borrowed. A contemporary drawing shows some of the myth surrounding Necker, who was believed to be a financial genius (60). By 1786 a new controller, Charles Alexandre de Calonne, had the idea of introducing a general land-tax, which would apply to all classes of society. An Assembly of Notables, chosen by the King, was summoned to meet at Versailles in 1787 and to signify its approval of this measure. The King attended the opening session on 22nd February, 1787 (61). But

60

61

faced with the opposition of the Notables, and under pressure from Marie-Antoinette, the King agreed to dismiss Calonne.

After the Notables, the King and Calonne's successor, Lomenie de Brienne, turned to the local assemblies, the Parlements. On 6th August, 1787, the King summoned the Parlement de Paris to Versailles and demanded that they register an edict creating new taxation.

The Parlement claimed that this was illegal, and demanded the summoning of the Estates-General. The King insisted that this was his right alone, and exiled them to Troyes.

In the provinces, violent support was given to the Parlement de Paris. At Grenoble the reaction went beyond violence. The Estates (Assembly) of the Province of Dauphiné were illegally convoked for the first time since 1628.

30 Picture (62) shows the Parlement de Paris in session in August, 1787. In a sense, therefore, the Revolution had begun with a revolt of the privileged. It was the aristocratic Parlements which had made people used to the idea of illegal assemblies and to violent resistance. The Church joined in and drew up its own Remonstrance. There was even a possible leader to the movement. The Duke of Orleans, the King's cousin, publicly protested against the King's action in November, 1787 (63). His protest was heard, but not heeded, and he was exiled to a nearby château. But the King capitulated. In August, 1788, Louis issued the announcement that the Estates-General would meet on 1st May, 1789, and Necker was called back to office.

As these crises had come alight, there was an immediate and sharp crisis brought about in the first instance by bad harvests. Heavy

rains had fallen in 1787, only to be followed by drought. A disastrous harvest in 1788, forced the price of bread dramatically high. The shortage of food was serious enough, but worse still there was added to it a panic fear of famine throughout France. It was a dangerous political situation which needed careful handling. Yet what could be done?

Since more money had to be spent on food, purchasing power slumped and industry began to suffer. Unemployment became widespread in the towns; food riots became a familiar feature in these months in town and country alike. In Paris, on 27th April, 1789, workmen sacked the house of a local manufacturer, by the name of Réveillon, because he was said to have spoken scathingly about their needs. The riot was brutally suppressed by the authorities (64), which only inflamed public feeling more, and heightened the growing frustration.

62

63

64

This agitation coincided with the expectations felt at the summoning of the Estates-General, and at the elections which were being organized; as a result, a political impact was given to all the various economic, administrative and social events. Paris, in particular, became a city of widespread gossip and speculation. The Duke of Orleans lived in the Palais-Royal and he probably encouraged this political discussion. The gardens of the Palais-Royal were a famous meeting-place (65). The young man on the right with hat in hand is the Duke of Orleans's son, the Duke of Chartres, who was to become King Louis-Philippe years after in 1830.

In September, 1788, the Parlement de Paris

65

66

returned triumphantly from exile to Paris. But it then destroyed its own popularity. While registering the declaration convoking the Estates-General it stated that it should be made up in the same way as when it last met. This had been generations before, in 1614 (67). The Church, nobility, and Third Estate had been equally represented. In December, 1788,

Necker proposed the doubling of the Third Estate. The "revolution of the privileged" had been defeated and, in spite of protests, it had ended. Necker and the King then enjoyed great popularity. A cartoon shows a Parisian craftsman and a washerwoman drinking to the health of the Third Estate (66). It was a momentous sign of the times.

67

CHAPTER TWO

TOWARDS THE BASTILLE

ONE OF THE GREATEST EFFECTS of the Enlightenment was to increase French self-consciousness. There was a sense of pessimism, a feeling that things could not continue without change. Sometimes current fears were expressed cynically; sometimes they were confused with the hopes of those groups who felt that the aristocracy had imposed a barrier on their progress. One revolutionary, Louis Antoine de Saint-Just, later stressed the fact that there was a new sentiment—conscious discontent. Even a distant observer like the Empress Maria Theresa of Austria seemed to feel that the situation was dangerous. She told her daughter, Marie-Antoinette, that she should put up with the boredom and the futility of the French court, otherwise she would have to face much more serious inconveniences than these petty burdens. The French, she said, were a touchy nation. Distant events also made men feel that change was in the air. The American War of Independence, the action of the Dutch Patriots in attacking the Prince of Orange, the revolt of the Austrian Netherlands, all provided practical examples of democratic ideas in action. If the French King could support American and Dutch republicans, then why should not new political ideas become fashionable? It was a time of experiment.

Of course, Louis XVI has had to bear a great deal of criticism from historians. He was not the man to face a real crisis. He had little energy and no determination; he could not see his way out of the many conflicting groups and coteries which surrounded him; he knew little about the kingdom which he was ruling and he had little understanding of what was going on. His only assets were his good intentions, and a vague bonhomie, which had given him a certain popularity among the population. It was unfortunate that his Queen should have helped to dispel it. Among Marie-Antoinette's more regrettable characteristics were her Austrian birth, a certain frivolity, a reputation for extravagance and a foolish ability to make enemies of important people.

Yet apart from the personal shortcomings of the king and his consort, it was perhaps the system of government which was most at fault. Theoretically, the king was the absolute monarch. He was responsible only to God, not to his subjects. If the affairs of government are divided into legislative, executive and judicial, it was the king who stood at the head of each. But, in practice, the government was not simply the king's government. To begin with, confusion reigned over the actual organization of administration. Since the death of Cardinal Fleury, there had been no single great minister. There was a chancellor, usually the keeper of the royal seal, a controller-general of finance, and four secretaries who concerned themselves with different subjects—War, the Marine,

Foreign Affairs and the Household. They attended the Council, as did the princes of the blood and other members of the nobility. The Council was presided over by the king and it debated all the affairs of the kingdom, leaving the actual decisions to the king. As business grew more complicated, and as the successor of Louis XIV did not always attend the Council, then other councils and committees took over certain of the tasks of the Council. Government became more technical; statistical services were established; officials saw to it that the holders of the great offices of state were better informed. But this mixture of the modern and the archaic made the situation of the king more uncertain.

It had always been difficult for the king to take action, even when the king had been Louis XIV. Absolutism had always been limited by traditional privileges. The system of centralization had never been completed. From medieval times onward the progress of the French king's power had often been matched by the power of other rulers—rulers whose feudal and provincial kingdoms lay within the frontiers of modern France. The French state had always been both strong and weak. A sign of its weakness was the absence of any uniform system of law. Written law and customary law, for example, existed side by side. There was no coherent system of administration—military, judicial, religious and economic organizations cut across one another throughout the kingdom. The effective importance of a bishop, of an intendant, of a noble, consequently varied from one part of France to another.

Since each official had bought and paid for his position, he had a certain independence from the royal authority. During the eighteenth century this independence

was demonstrated by the *parlementaires*. There were thirteen Parlements, the biggest of which (the Parlement de Paris) covered more than a third of all France. These Parlements were courts of law, which also had the right to register the decrees and edicts of the king. After the death of Louis XIV they began to assert their independent authority; they disputed with the Church and became kernels of opposition to the royal will. The *parlementaires* formed a rich and exclusive class; having paid for their offices, they could not be dispossessed; hostile towards absolutism they embraced some of the ideas of the Enlightenment.

This, then, was the paradox of the French monarchy—all-powerful and at the same time powerless. Significantly, power had not yet devolved upon any other section of society. There might be much opposition to royal absolutism, yet that opposition was still profoundly monarchist. If the bourgeoisie were anti-aristocratic and wanted to break open the world of aristocratic privilege, they nevertheless did not want to depend too much upon the king. Within the Parlements, the aristocracy and sections of the Third Estate sometimes collaborated. If the aristocracy were becoming more exacting over their rights and more punctilious over their privileges, many became indifferent to a hierarchical and obsolescent society. Indeed, without the aristocracy, their salons, their role in the discussion groups and society, there might have been no Enlightenment at all.

It was hard for contemporaries to see in what direction the French state was moving. The great nineteenth-century French historian, François Guizot, said that the Revolution was a violent way of breaking out of the *ancien régime*.

There were those who, well before 14th July, 1789, talked about a "French Revolution." By this they meant the summoning of the Estates-General. There can be no doubt that the elections and the compilation of grievances in the local *cahiers de doléances* (books of grievances) created great excitement. The bourgeois in the towns demanded equality of status with the privileged. The peasants wanted a reduction of dues and other exactions;

many bourgeois and aristocrats looked forward to some sort of a limited monarchy governing with the Estates.

On 4th May, 1789, the Estates-General met at Versailles and went in procession to hear Mass (68). The next day the historic opening session was held, at which Necker read a long and technical speech on the financial situation (69). The Third Estate was disappointed to find that only technical problems were en-

68

69

visaged, rather than major reforms. It was humiliating and frustrating for them that the three orders had to sit separately. In June, tiring of these procedural arguments, the Third Estate proclaimed itself the National Assembly and invited the other orders to join them. Their President was Jean Bailly, the famous astronomer (70). On 20th June, owing to a muddle, the Third Estate found itself locked out of its meeting-place. Indignantly,

the members retired to an indoor tennis-court and passed a resolution not to adjourn until a constitution had been made. Bailly read this resolution, often known as the Tennis Court Oath (72). In front of him we see the monk Dom Gerle, the Abbé Grégoire and the pastor Rabaut Saint-Étienne. By the end of the month many nobles and clergy had joined the Third Estate. The unity of the orders had become a subject for rejoicing (71).

70

71

72

These events, together with the high price of bread, had maintained a turmoil in Paris. It was in this atmosphere that Louis's court decided it was strong enough to take action. On 11th July, Necker was dismissed by the King and sent into exile. When this was known in Paris on the next day, a Sunday, there were immediate protests and violence (73). The Parisians set up their own municipal guard to protect the city against the royal army. An engraving (74) shows a night patrol of Paris guards with torches, looking to the security of the city, on the night of 12th–13th July, 1789.

On 14th July, still in search of arms, the Parisians invaded a great city arsenal, the Invalides. Inside the gates, they overcame resistance, and seized four cannon and no less than 32,000 rifles. Using the cannon taken from the Invalides, and with the help of some sympathetic soldiers, they attacked the ancient

73

74

fortress-prison of the Bastille (75). After a rather amateur attack of five hours, it finally surrendered. To the victors, it was a great symbol of defiance against the authority of the *ancien régime*. In fact, the real value of the event was small. The Bastille only held seven prisoners, two of whom were confined because they were mad. It was not much of a prize, but the triumph of the Parisians was linked with the idea of liberation, and the freed prisoners were escorted in a victory parade through the streets (76). One (on the right) is carried on a litter. More real, however, was the demand for vengeance. It was claimed that the authorities had promised to give arms, and then had opened fire on the crowd. Jacques de Flesselles, Provost of Merchants, was killed for having supposedly been an accomplice (77). He was later decapitated, and his head was carried on a pike through the streets.

75

76

77

Louis XVI gave way: he recalled Necker. On 17th July the King went with a number of deputies to the Hôtel de Ville (city hall) of Paris, where he was received with honour (79). Bailly, whom he had just nominated Mayor, gave him the cockade (hat badge) of red and blue, the colours of the city. Together with white for the House of Bourbon, this was to be the national cockade. The King was loudly cheered for wearing the cockade which Bailly had given him. Paris was in need of symbols.

But this did not stop violence. On 22nd July, a member of the ministry which had temporarily replaced Necker, Foullon de Dové, was seized and within a short time executed. He had been in charge of food supplies, and was widely blamed for the critical food shortage.

The cry from the mob was, "Foullon à la

78

79

80

lanterne!" ("Hang Foullon from the lamp!") The mob took Foullon to a street corner, and hanged him on the 23rd July (80). The rope broke twice and the victim's wretched agony was prolonged.

The Marquis de Lafayette was made Commander of the National Guard in Paris. A famous cartoon (78) shows Lafayette paying court to "Madame Bailly," while her husband, Lafayette's colleague as Mayor, looks on.

Much of France turned to Paris for leadership, and imitated her conduct. Municipal revolutions broke out in many towns—Dijon, Rouen, Bordeaux, Lyons and elsewhere. National Guards were formed in local areas, and sometimes armed themselves with weapons seized from the army. In Strasbourg, the Hôtel de Ville was sacked.

In the countryside the second half of July saw a general breakdown of social order and discipline. The collapse of royal authority in the towns contributed to this event. Dues were not paid; châteaux, manor-houses and abbeys were attacked; game was taken illegally; common lands were restored; manorial rolls and feudal records were burned (81).

In all this, lay an element of collective panic, known as the *grande peur* (great fear). Fear grew in the provinces as harvest-time drew near. Regular troops and National Guards were sent out to repress these disturbances (82).

So it was that the revolution of the privileged orders was followed by the revolution of the Third Estate and of the towns, and followed by the revolution of the countryside. Where was it all to stop? A solution other than force was proposed in the National Assembly by the Duke of Aiguillon, and by the Viscount of

81

82   83

Noailles: abolish all feudal privileges. The aristocratic and landowning class was divided, but the feudal régime was nevertheless abolished. A commemorative medal was made of the event (83). Bishops' mitres and symbols of the nobility were destroyed by revolutionaries (85). This was a political calculation as much as a movement of exultation. After 4th August, feudal rights which were in the nature of property rather than of personal servitude were made redeemable. The following day a great memorial service was held in Notre-Dame Cathedral for those who had died in the storming of the Bastille (84).

On 26th August, the Assembly passed its historic vote of the Rights of Man, gaining the admiration of a whole host of reformers, including the English radical, Tom Paine (86), who published *The Rights of Man* in support of the Revolution in 1791.

84
85

86

The National Assembly had accomplished much, but France still had to establish a constitution. The difficulty was that the King was uncooperative, and many of the nobility were utterly hostile. The Duke of Orleans (87) continued his plots, and many felt that if he became king, there could be a reconciliation with the monarchy.

Fears of a counter-revolution were height-ened by the strengthening of the army at Versailles. On 1st October, at a private banquet in the opera house at Versailles (89), army officers loudly cheered the royal family and wore the white cockades of the Bourbons. The fears of Paris were quickly aroused; it was like the dismissal of Necker all over again.

When the news of the dinner was known on 3rd October, 1789, a variety of measures were

87

88

89

9
9

proposed by Parisian leaders. The next day, a Sunday, it was suggested that there should be a march to Versailles to bring the King back to Paris. Assembling rather mysteriously on a rainy 5th October, some 5,000 or 6,000 women, most of them poor, but including some bourgeoises, set off for Versailles, outside Paris. They were armed with pikes and with two cannon (88). After killing some of the royal bodyguard and seizing supplies of flour, and being joined by the National Guard, deputies of the Third Estate and immense crowds, the women returned in triumph to Paris, bringing the King with them (90). The mob was quickly learning its power. The King settled in the Tuileries Palace (91). He had left Versailles for good. From that moment onward, Paris dominated the Revolution.

CHAPTER THREE

THE FIRST REPUBLIC

"THE KING is in the Louvre, the National Assembly is at the Tuileries, the corn-mills are grinding, the traitors are in full flight, the patriots have triumphed." So wrote Camille Desmoulins, Robespierre's friend, in October, 1790. He was not alone in thinking that the Revolution had been completed. True, a constitution had still to be devised, but surely this would not prove difficult. After all, the deputies believed in the power of reason; man would recognize the highest good when he saw it. Order had been restored, the threat of military counter-revolution had been met and overcome, the harvest had been good. Nothing could stop the Assembly, meeting in the converted riding-school of the Tuileries, from proceeding rationally in its work, and uniting the Church, the aristocracy and the people (92). The Duke of Orleans, the source of much rumour and conspiracy, had sailed to England; several of the more aristocratically inclined deputies had not joined their colleagues in the move from Versailles. Popular enthusiasm was felt for both Assembly and King, and cries of "Vive le Roi!" had mingled with "Vive la Nation!" The decision of 4th August, and the Declaration of the Rights of Man, had swept away the past and abolished forever the aristocratic monopoly of power and privilege. The Revolution was complete.

Yet, the Revolution continued. Why was this? For some, it was because the deputies of the National Assembly had underestimated the power of the counter-revolution. In September, 1789, the King's brother, the Comte d'Artois, settled in Turin, and began to prepare to overthrow what had been accomplished. In October, the King was already being urged to flee eastward. Aristocratic resistance had been underestimated: although the counter-revolution was to become as diverse and heterogeneous as the Revolution itself, and shot through with myth, it can be maintained that the Revolution was never really secure. The weakest part of the settlement which existed in October, 1789, and which would persist until 1791, was Louis XVI himself. Indecisive and negative he may have been, yet he was at heart a determined enemy of the National Assembly. He believed in the *ancien régime*. Surrounded by powerful enemies, the Revolution had no choice but to keep moving forward from one stage on to another.

Others have seen things in a different light. For them, revolution of any kind is a slippery slope. Once the first steps have been taken, it is difficult, even impossible, to call a halt. Just as the privileged orders in the Parlements and Estates had started —with the summoning of the Estates-General—a movement which they could

92

not stop, so the middle-class lawyers and officials in the National Assembly had also begun something they could not control. Once the mob had tasted power, as in July and October of 1789, its appetite grew. A revolutionary mentality had developed, and now, with the Assembly meeting in the excitable atmosphere of Paris, the scope for extremist agitation was even greater. Seen in this light, the Revolution was doomed to roll further down the slope. Some have claimed that it has never stopped. Talleyrand remarked to the Academy in 1836, "The French Revolution, which still continues . . ."

Here was the paradox. The Declaration of the Rights of Man was a statement of individualism. It asserted that there were fundamental human rights: freedom from arbitrary arrest and imprisonment, freedom of opinion, freedom of speech, freedom from taxation without consent. The right of property was stated to be natural and sacred. Equality of rights was emphasized, including equality before the law and equality of opportunity. But at the same time it was an authoritarian government. "The source of all authority resides essentially in the nation," stated the Declaration. Many of the rights which are affirmed exist in the interests of society as a whole. The supremacy of the law is clearly stated. All this means that instead of having a society ruled over by a monarch responsible to God alone, but where authority is tempered by a considerable mass of traditions and privileges, there will be a society where a representative assembly has power that is unrestricted and complete, even totalitarian.

While the Assembly theorized about the sovereignty of the people, in practice the deputies would not share political power with the lower classes. In the new constitution of 1791, a distinction was drawn between "active" and "passive" citizens. All adult males were citizens, but only those who paid in direct taxes the equivalent of three days work, annually, were active citizens with the right of voting. There was an even higher property qualification for those who could sit in the national parliament. Thus a new in-equality was created. In some ways the Revolution was bound to continue. The fact that it was insecure, or the fact that it was incomplete, made it inevitable that it should move on. But one must beware of investing these confused moments of French history with too much order.

In local affairs the nation of France was divided into eighty-three departments, each department into districts, and every town and parish was established as a "commune." Each "commune" and district became responsible for its public life, and officials and assemblies were to be elected at various levels. But the complexity of all these regulations, the frequency of elections, and in particular the absence of any provision for financing local government, led to considerable confusion and to endless recrimination. Political societies and clubs took on a particular importance. With an Assembly in the middle which was deadlocked and with an uncertain democratic experiment taking place throughout the country, there was little sense of stability. Of crucial importance was the Assembly's decision to confiscate the lands of the Church. The financial crisis that had necessitated the calling of the Estates-General still persisted; normal means of raising money failed and therefore the extraordinary way, that of considering that Church property belonged to the general community of believers, was adopted. In order to facilitate this sale of perhaps one-fifth of the land of France, interest-bearing bonds called *assignats* were issued, redeemable either in land or in the proceeds of its sale. In 1790 these *assignats* became legal tender. From these measures came the conflict between the Revolution and the Catholics and the existence of a devaluing paper currency. Then there was the war. By 1792 many felt that a war against other European monarchies, probably a short and mild war, would be a means of resolving France's political problems. There were many different expectations, but war was seen as a remedy. The war that was fought was very different from that which had been imagined. The Revolution was transformed.

48 The National Assembly met in the converted riding-school at the Tuileries: would the King agree to be a constitutional monarch? In the palace, the King and Queen and their entourage (97) did not conceal their hostility to the Assembly, and its plans for a new constitution.

The outstanding orator of the Assembly was Honoré Riqueti de Mirabeau (94). He was the principal member of the Third Estate for Aix-en-Provence. From October, 1789, his personal ambition was to replace Necker as the chief minister. But from May, 1790, he was in the pay of the court. He died in April, 1791. Antoine Barnave (98) was Mirabeau's rival. He fought to stabilize and unite the Revolution with the King. He was to be executed during the Terror, in November, 1793. A cartoon of Barnave shows him both as a man of the court and a man of the people (95).

93

94

95 96

Outside the Assembly, much political activity took place, focused particularly in the new political clubs in Paris. The Abbé Sieyès (93), deputy for Paris, founded a 1789 Society, but it was very expensive and exclusive. In April, 1789, the Breton deputies to the Estates-General founded a club at Versailles. In December they founded another club—the Jacobin Club—in a disused Dominican monastery in Paris. The Jacobins, as the members were called, became famous for the directness of their discussions. By 1790, the club had 1,100 members, in France, and its political influence was to become very great. A wide spectrum of political opinions was seen. The Jacobins were to become identified with the Revolution itself. Figure (99) shows the interior of the Jacobin Club. The President is Charles de Lameth, the speaker Mirabeau. Picture (96) portrays a Jacobin caricatured as a bourgeois.

97

98

99

In addition to the clubs, many newspapers were also politically active, enjoying a new liberty of the Press: there were 150 newspapers in 1791. One famous newspaper-owner was Camille Desmoulins (100), a lawyer who first became famous when he harangued the crowds in the Palais-Royal after Necker's dismissal in 1789. His newspaper, *Révolutions de France et de Brabant*, represented left-wing opinions. Jean-Paul Marat (101) founded the newspaper *L'Ami du Peuple* in September, 1789, noted for its attacks on the Assembly and support for ordinary people. Marat was also the founder of the "Society of the Rights of Man and of the Citizen." From April, 1790, this club met at the Convent of the Cordeliers (102).

The National Guard had been formed in the spring and summer of 1789 to defend the Assembly against aristocratic plots. Later, it protected the Revolution against pressure from

100

101

102

103

the left. It was recruited from the richer citizens. Lafayette (103) was its Commander-in-chief. An aristocrat, he was one of the idols of Paris but was regarded as unreliable. He sought to become the political leader during 1790. Mirabeau nicknamed him "simple-Caesar." Disturbances arose in many parts of France, and National Guards were often used to restore order. In Montauban, on 10th May, 1790, an affray rose from counter-revolution-ary activity. The National Guard was attacked by Catholics (104). In August, 1790, a pay dispute led to a revolt in a regiment at Nancy. The National Guard in Metz marched there, and repressed it with heavy casualties, and the whole affair became an anti-Jacobin issue. A ceremony was held for the citizen-soldiers who had died (105). André Desilles, a lieutenant who tried to prevent bloodshed between the soldiers, was killed (106), some said martyred.

105

104   106

A great effort was made to maintain the enthusiasm of the Revolution. Trees of liberty were planted with much ceremony in cities and villages; in the different towns of France as in the different districts of Paris, oaths were solemnly sworn "to the Nation, the Law and the King." The citizens of the Saint-Étienne du Mont district of Paris swore their oath in February, 1790, in a crowded square, with soldiers drawn up on parade (107).

A great ceremony was organized for 14th July, 1790, when all the National Guards of France were to assemble to take the oath. The elaborate preparations on the Champ-de-Mars in Paris, where the ceremony was to be held, were running late; the ordinary people, and leaders such as Lafayette, went there to help carry out the work and ensure that every-

107

108

109

thing would be ready for the event (108, 109). This Fête de la Fédération (110) was the greatest of all the revolutionary festivals. Thousands of Parisians gathered in the stands to watch the military march past; cannon fired salutes. It was a popular event and launched the idea of celebrating 14th July each year (112). Bastille Day had become the great symbol of the Revolution, and would always be celebrated in succeeding generations.

It was also a religious festival. After a Mass celebrated by Talleyrand, Bishop of Autun, Lafayette took the oath at a mystical "Altar of the Fatherland" (111), cheered by the vast crowds surrounding the special dais, guarded by lines of soldiers. To everyone there, it must have been a stirring occasion, and a deeply impressive one.

110

111

112

54 It could be said that the festival of 14th July, 1790 (114), represented the tradition of the Estates-General. With Talleyrand and Lafayette, the old idea was present that the three orders were joining together in creating a new constitution acceptable to all, as a contemporary cartoon suggests (113).

It was argument about finance which broke this harmony. This was a long-standing problem. Efforts were made to increase the revenue by any means possible, including "patriotic gifts" by the people. An engraving shows a group of actresses presenting gifts to the Assembly in September, 1789 (115).

The idea that the property of the Church belonged to all believers (not just priests), and that it could be used by the nation, was first developed by Talleyrand. This remarkable

113

114

115

man, Bishop of Autun and an aristocrat, was to show great skill in moving with the times.

The property of the Church was put at the disposal of the nation in November, 1789. The state now became responsible for the organization of the Church; it gave the Church a civil constitution, whereby bishops and curés were to be elected. In November, 1790, an oath of loyalty to the regime was imposed on all priests. One-third of the priests refused to take this oath. In March, 1791, the Pope condemned the civil constitution; an ideological breach had appeared in the Revolution, and feeling ran high against the Church. On 6th April, 1791, an effigy of the Pope was burned in the gardens of the Palais-Royal (117), and in July the remains of Voltaire were glorified in Paris in a festival of anti-clericalism (116).

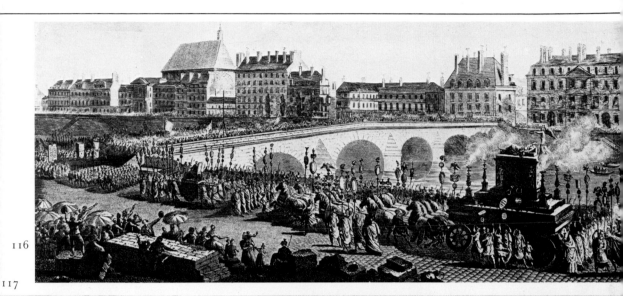

116

117

The sale of Church property was a complicated matter. To make things easier, the government in December, 1789, created a new series of interest-earning Treasury bonds. These bonds were not successful with the public. In April, 1790, the interest was reduced; they were made legal tender, and became a new paper currency.

The political aim was to create a class of people who had a financial interest in the Revolution. The monetary aim was to stimulate the economy. In fact by 1791 these actions had begun a cycle of depreciation and inflation. The *assignats* (119, 120), as the bonds were called, impeded the natural progress of economic life. By the spring of 1791 widespread anxiety was felt. This political and ideological unrest was intensified by a rise in

prices and an increase in the number of unemployed. Distrust of the royal family became a focal point of this discontent. Mirabeau died suddenly in April, 1791. He is supposed to have said as he died, "I carry in my heart the funeral knell of the monarchy." He was given a state funeral in the French capital (118).

At this moment, Louis XVI decided to escape from Paris and set up the royal standard in the east. He planned to travel to Metz, where the Marquis de Bouillé (121) after cruelly suppressing the rebels at Nancy, was in control of reliable troops. The King and Queen made their way from the Tuileries Palace on 20th June. Marie-Antoinette disguised herself as a governess working for the Baroness Korff. In reality Baroness Korff was Madame de Tourzel, governess of the royal children (122).

119

120

18

121

122

The King was recognized, and late in the evening, in the small town of Varennes, he was forced to go to the house of the local magistrate, Monsieur Sance (125). There he admitted his true identity. He clung to the hope that Bouillé would rescue him, but he was forced to start his journey back to Paris. Bouillé arrived two hours too late.

The English cartoonist Gillray claimed that the National Assembly was worried by news of the King's flight, and elated by news of his recapture (127). Illustrations of the time show the King being recognized in his carriage (123).

Once back in Paris, the King was held prisoner and suspended from his functions. But the Assembly, believing still that a king

ARESTATION·DU ROI·ET·DE·SA·FAMILLE A·VARENNE

L'arrestation du Roi a eu lieu à Varennes, à cinq lieues de France, vers une heure après minuit, au moment où l'on venait d'en être prévenu par M. Drouet, maître de poste de Sainte-Menehould, qui a rendu un service essentiel à la France, qu'elle surprise pour les fugitifs de se voir arrêtés au milieu de la nuit, par deux braves gardes nationaux

LA RÉCOMPENCE ACORDÉE A Mr DROUET EST DE 30 MILLE LIVRE ET A Mr SAUCE 20 MILLE LIVRE

qui ont br traître lui et a

123

124

125

was needed, accepted the fiction that the King had been obliged by others to take the action that he did. Even the Jacobin Club was ready to accept the fiction that the King had been kidnapped. A demonstration was organized on the Champ-de-Mars to protest against this policy, and demand action. By a sad accident, the protest became violent. Martial law was quickly proclaimed, and the red flag of revolution displayed (124). Lafayette ordered the National Guard to fire on the people (126), and some fifteen people were killed. The "massacre" of the Champ-de-Mars, as it came to be known, represented a split in the Third Estate: what ought the relations between King, Assembly and people to be?

menaces d'un détachement de hussards, qui avoit été commandé par le
! M Sauce, Procureur de la Commune, a invité ? Roi d'entrer chez
reposer lui et sa famille Le généreux citoyen de Varennes n'a point
s offres du Roi. d'sont qu'il devoit tout à sa patrie.

126

127

60

For Antoine Barnave, and for others, the time had come to assert that the Revolution had achieved its aims. The Assembly had to be dissolved; the new constitution had to be proclaimed, and the new Legislative Assembly had to begin its work of reconstruction. So it was, that on 3rd September, 1791, the constitution (128) was signed by the King, and on 13th September it was publicly proclaimed in the streets of Paris (131). Medals (129, 130) were struck, and cockades appeared in honour of the new constitution.

The Legislative Assembly met for the first time on 1st October, 1791. By law, members of the old Assembly were disqualified from sitting in it. The country, deeply divided

128

DÉCRET DE L'ASSEMBLÉE NATIONALE.

129,130

among itself, was ruled by a new constitution and by new men.

In the Assembly one of the men who was to become most influential was Jean-Pierre Brissot (132). A journalist who could claim friendship with the most radical as well as with the conservative aristocrats such as Lafayette, he was the focus of a group of active people who combined great idealism with capacity for intrigue. This group included Pierre-Victorin Vergniaud, the greatest orator of his age (133). It also numbered in its ranks Madame Roland (134) the attractive and ambitious wife of Jean-Marie Roland (135), an official from Lyons. This group became known as the Brissotins.

One of the main points of Brissotin policy was to fight the counter-revolution which was growing against France in Europe. Brissot believed that it was fundamental for France to attack Austria, Prussia and other courts in Europe which were aiding the *émigrés*. In Europe the Revolution had had a sort of popularity. It had seemed to be a rational organization of government. Englishmen had agreed to accept honours from the revolutionaries. The Paris Commune for example in January, 1790, presented a Mr. C. J. W. Nesham from England with a civic crown and a sword (136).

Edmund Burke (137), however, condemned the Revolution and prophesied disaster for it, in his famous work *Reflections on the Revolution in France* (November, 1790). An English cartoon (139) depicts a citizen uneasily placed on the debris of social order. To the right the people are presented with *assignats* instead of food,

136

137

138

and a severed head instead of laws; to the left there are wars in the name of peace and violence in the name of humanity.

The countries of Europe were not united against France. The Czarina of Russia, Catherine (140), was more interested in eastern Europe. In England, William Pitt (141) was more concerned with Canada and with the English colonies. All the war initiative came from the French. Louis XVI hoped for an in-vasion which would rescue him from his sub-jects; Lafayette hoped that a short European conflict would enable the generals to stabilize the situation; Brissot believed that war would stimulate the economy and consolidate the Revolution. When an adventurer, Charles Dumouriez (138) became Minister of Foreign Affairs in March, 1792, war became more likely. Dumouriez was in contact with the King, seeking war for private ambition.

139

140

141

64 On 20th April, 1792, the Assembly approved a declaration of war against Austria. Robespierre (145), believed that the counter-revolution existed, not in central Europe, but within the boundaries of France herself. He saw the war as merely a political move by Lafayette. Robespierre was concerned with the rising cost of living and with the situation of the poor, and took a prominent part in the celebration of the revolutionary martyrs of Nancy (142). A counter-demonstration was organized by Brissot and the moderates in memory of Simoneau, Mayor of Étampes, who was killed in a food riot in March, 1792. Brissot's demonstration (144), took place in June under the famous banner *Liberté, égalité, fraternité* (Liberty, equality, brotherhood). Inside France, a revolutionary cult (of Robespierrists) had come face to face with a bourgeois cult (of Brissotins).

143   142

The political struggle was fought against the background of the war and against the failure of the French army to take any effective action. After much hesitation, in May and June, the Brissotins issued decrees against non-juror priests (priests who refused the constitutional oath of loyalty); they abolished the King's personal guard and set up a permanent camp of 20,000 National Guards near Paris. The King vetoed the first and last of these decrees, an unpopular action, as shown by a cartoon which urges the people to attack the King, Monsieur Veto (143).

Joseph Pétion (146) was elected Mayor of Paris in November, 1791. He arranged that the crowd should be allowed to enter the Tuileries Palace, thinking that this would help the Brissotins and his own popularity. Antoine Joseph Santerre (147), a wealthy brewer, was becoming the real leader of the Paris mob.

144

145

146,147

66 A coloured engraving, first published soon after the Revolution, shows the people forcing their way into the Tuileries (148). In a famous incident, the King was made to put on the traditional red bonnet of the Revolution (149). By his composure, however, he saved the situation, and he was left unharmed.

It seemed at this time that the danger of counter-revolution was the greatest threat to France. As the Prussian and Austrian armies prepared to cross the frontiers of France, National Guards began to converge on Paris. The most famous National Guardsmen were the volunteers from Marseilles who marched on Paris singing their famous song, the "Marseillaise," which had been composed by Rouget de L'Isle. A song sheet illustrates the scene (150).

149

148

150

MARCHE DES MARSEILLOIS
CHANTÉE SUR DIFERANS THEATRES
Chez Frere Passage du Saumon

After the Prussians had made their declaration of war, the French Assembly proclaimed a state of emergency on 11th July. The proclamation *La Patrie en danger!* (The Country in danger!) was issued throughout France, and was a call to arms. A military parade was held in Paris (151), and enrolment places (on the right in the picture) were set up for volunteers. France was to have the first truly national army which the peoples of Europe had ever seen.

Unity was not complete however. When the Marseillais arrived in Paris, Santerre invited them to a patriotic banquet in the Champs-Élysées. This degenerated into a violent clash (152) between the Marseillais and other National Guards from the west of France who were personal supporters of the Marquis de Lafayette.

151

152

News of the proclamation of the Duke of Brunswick (155) became known in Paris around 1st August. In it, the allied commander bluntly declared that Their Majesties Francis II of Austria and Frederick William of Prussia meant to end the prevailing anarchy in France, and restore royal authority. A French cartoon (153) shows the allied sovereigns preparing to blow up the noisy Assembly, and reflects some of the French fears which were felt with regard to national security.

But the Assembly was far from ready for violent action. It refused to support a move to impeach Lafayette, Commander of the National Guard, nor would it consider deposing the King. Many Parisians felt deep

153

frustration at this. The insurrection that was started on the night of 9th August was directed against the King, the Assembly, and foreign powers alike. On the following day, 10th August, 1792, an angry mob attacked the Tuileries Palace (154, 156). It was a fearful and bloody occasion. In the frenzied rioting and shooting, the situation rapidly escalated, and got completely out of control. More than a thousand people were killed—shot or trampled underfoot. But the mob had its way, and the King himself was taken prisoner.

The 10th August was the democratic and patriotic revolution, within the French Revolution. Very soon, the King was to be stripped of all his powers as anti-royalism in Paris grew.

154 155

156

CHAPTER FOUR

THE TERROR

THE FRANCE which went to war was a country rich in manpower; she also had varied agriculture and boasted relatively good means of communication. Nowhere did there stand one dominant site of industrial or commercial wealth which, if captured, would constitute an irreparable loss. But, as we have seen, France was liable to agricultural crises which had their effect on industry. A rise in the price of bread reduced the purchasing power of all consumers; textile production suffered, and so brought increasing distress to the town populations whose livelihood it was. Interruption of the normal channels of trade, whether through apprehension and fear, foreign invasion, or economic discouragement, could also produce bad effects on the economy as a whole and on the town-dwellers in particular.

All these phenomena were present during 1792. The harvest of 1791 had been only fair; peasants were not prepared to sell their food in return for a rapidly depreciating paper currency. Disturbances in different parts of the country interrupted normal communications. In addition, the revolt in the West Indian island of San Domingo cut off sugar supplies. The invasion of France by enemy troops, and the need to organize food supplies and materials for the French army, disrupted ordinary economic life. These same conditions were to be reproduced, often with a greater intensity, in 1793, when the rising in the Vendée, for

example, affected communications between Nantes and Paris. The effect of this was clear enough: the liberal, bourgeois experiment in government was finished. There were those who demanded control of the economy, to force people to sell on the open market, regulate prices and check speculation. There would have to be an increase in governmental power and activity.

At the same time, France risked defeat in the war. This would be more than a national defeat, such as might happen to any eighteenth-century state or dynasty. It would be a defeat for the forces of the Revolution, and a victory for the forces of counter-revolution. To meet this menace, two things were needed: a great volunteer movement, in which the populations (mainly urban) would show their enthusiasm for the Revolution by enlisting; and a governmental assault on all those who felt sympathy for the enemy and the counter-revolution. Greater democracy, as it were, should go hand in hand with the greater state authority. France, therefore, was to enter a period of "totalitarian democracy."

France was destined to be at war for some twenty-three years (although the character of the wars was to change). War was a great simplifier. Those who wanted the monarchy restored were sometimes prepared to see this effected by means of a national defeat: therefore they were traitors. Those who believed in the

Revolution were sometimes prepared to protect it by every means. At moments of crisis it was impossible to find compromise positions.

It is in the light of this situation that one should examine Robespierre, who has long been a figure of controversy among historians. For some, he represents everything that was worst in the Revolution. He was the classic fanatic and extremist who appears in every revolt, the one who commits the most atrocious crimes in the name of humanity and who will stop at nothing to maintain his hold on power. For others, he was one of the most lucid leaders of the Revolution. Not only did he understand what was happening, and what would happen, more clearly than most (he foresaw the consequences of Brissot's enthusiasm for war, for example), he also tried to determine policy within a framework of theory. He attempted to dominate events and to decide the direction in which the Revolution was moving. Yet others see Robespierre as one of the series of politicians catapulted into power by the Revolution, and broken before he had time to work out his ideas or his doctrine. Robespierre, seen in this way, is less corrupt than Danton, less superficial than Brissot, less imbued by bitterness than Marat, but he is in no way more significant than any of them or than many of their associates.

In fact, we should understand how someone like Robespierre evolved. As a moderately successful lawyer, and as one of the ablest members of the National Assembly, Robespierre had stood for many of the principles of 1789. He was essentially humanitarian, he believed in the goodness of man, he thought that society would progress if it was given freedom. Forced to lead a great witch-hunt, he inspired the Terror, because of what had happened to the Revolution itself. It had become caught up in a national emergency, and the very nature of the emergency had illuminated the differences that existed among the supporters of the Revolution. The Jacobin Club, on the whole represented a prosperous section of the community which, whether by interest or conviction believed in government by the wealthy, and economy based upon profit and a free society. The *sans-culottes* ("men without fine breeches") on the other hand, who came to dominate the forty-eight Paris Sections, and who formed much of the army, represented the urban population. This population was neither wealthy and bourgeois, nor poor and proletarian. These artisans, shop-keepers, and clerical workers wanted a different form of state. Robespierre's task was to create harmony among these divergent groups and interests.

After experience of twentieth-century warfare, with its "fifth columns" and its "enemy within," we should understand the Terror better than nineteenth-century historians. It was not a blind blood-letting; it was a means of ensuring unity and security. Naturally there was suspicion of traitors, since there really was treason, just as there really was corruption. We must beware of seeing the different groups as united and organized political parties. There were groups of friends, personalities, an awareness of various interests. Always, too, was the idea that state affairs ought to be directed according to the general will of the people. How this should be done led to controversy and bitterness. But at no time did Frenchmen lose their real aspirations—that the Revolution would one day make France a better place, and give men a higher moral stature.

72

After the insurrection of 10th August, the King was removed from all his functions, and the people of Paris gave themselves over to an orgy of anti-royalism.

The statue of Louis XIV which stood in the Place des Victoires was pulled down and smashed (157). Riots and attacks on property grew more and more frequent. In these danger-ous times, many deputies failed to attend the sessions of the Legislative Assembly. Liberal Jacobins—followers of Brissot, or deputies from the Gironde province (Girondins)— con-tinued to exercise control. They sought to allay popular excitement by appointing Georges Danton (161) as Minister of Justice. The son of a lawyer of Arcis, in Champagne, Danton was

interested in money. He was also an energetic leader of the left.

Today, Danton remains a difficult man to understand. More typical of the Girondins was Marguerite-Elie Guadet (158), a lawyer from Saint-Emilion: this was a man with great qualities, but who was also capable of much pettiness. François Buzot (159), the *porte-parole* (spokesman) of Madame Roland, sought to emphasize her likes and dislikes. He was later to become prominent in the Convention.

The Paris Commune, an elective body representing the Parisian activists, was a power rivalling the Assembly. There were new figures, here, too including Collot d'Herbois (160) a former actor, and Jean Tallien (162).

158

159

160

57

161

162

From 13th August, 1792, the guillotine stood in a prominent position in the Place du Carrousel. Little time was to be passed before it began to rise and fall. This instrument (163) is often thought to be the invention of Dr. Joseph Ignace Guillotin (164) a revolutionary politician who had been a member of the Third Estate. In fact, he was responsible only for suggesting that it be used in order to reduce the suffering of those who were due for execution. Since the blade fell from a considerable height, it fulfilled its function swiftly and effectively. Robespierre (165), a member of the Commune and an influential member of the Jacobin Club, did not himself organize the 10th August movement. But he apprehended the danger of isolating the bourgeoisie from the people. His importance to the future of

163

164

165

events was undeniable. He hoped to be a unifying factor, while still emphasizing the mission of the Revolution.

The counter-revolution was not always successful. In the southeast, the revolutionaries recaptured the town of Jalès (166), which the European enemy had taken at the beginning of the war. But elsewhere the invaders continued their advance. In August, the town of

Longwy was forced to surrender to the Austrians, Prussians and *émigrés*. In September it was the turn of Verdun (168). On both occasions there were widespread reports of treason, especially in Verdun, where the commanding officer Nicolas Beaurepaire died in mysterious circumstances. The call to patriots to fight was intensified as the foreign threat to the Revolution alarmed French opinion more.

75

166

167

168

Danton appeared as the man of the hour, and appealed to France for daring war measures. It was now decided to send a massive army to the front; the tocsin (alarm) began to sound, and a massacre of foreign and French royalist prisoners was launched in Paris. An engraving depicts one such event, a number of which took place between 2nd and 6th September, 1792 (169). One of the most famous incidents concerned the Princess Lamballe. When she refused to renounce her loyalty to the King she was struck down and killed, and horribly mutilated. Her head was stuck on the end of a pike, and then displayed to political prisoners in the Temple Prison (170). In the Abbey of Saint-Germain-des-Pres, a number of non-juror (anti-revolutionary) priests were executed by the orders of a popular tribunal set up by the lawyer Stanislas Maillard (171).

These September massacres, as they came

169

170

to be known, cost the lives of some 2,000 people. They were carried out by the petty bourgeois and artisans. Some incidents, such as the killing of prisoners at Versailles (172) were accompanied by uncontrolled robbery and pillaging. In an atmosphere of such violence in the streets, no one could feel entirely safe.

The world disapproved strongly of such happenings. English cartoons had already depicted satirically the so-called "limited" French monarchy (174) and the crushing embrace of unlimited French democracy (175). It seemed to be a strange contrast. Another engraving shows the devil's better half bringing the Jacobins into the world, to the horror and stupefaction of the devil himself (173). Many foreign observers who had once praised the idealism of the Revolution, now began seriously to doubt its true nature.

171

172

173

174

175

On 20th September, 1792, the French won a sudden victory over the Prussians at Valmy. The Prussians, surprised, withdrew. The legend of the French soldier (176), and of France as a nation in arms, was born.

On the same day, the meeting was held of a new Assembly (the Convention), elected by less than a tenth of the electors. The Jacobins, sitting in the highest seats of the Manège (the converted riding-school), were called the Mountain. They were reinforced by the presence of a Robespierre supporter, Jean Billaud-Varennes. But neither they nor any group were able to dominate the meeting. It was the Plain (the uncommitted moderates) which had the majority, led by men like Bertrand Barère (177).

The Convention was soon torn apart by disagreements. Outside, the Paris Sections showed their lack of confidence in any form of

176

177

178

180

179

parliamentary government; inside, there was whispered gossip of dictatorship. One of the subjects of disagreement was the King. What should be done with him? Should he be impeached for crimes against the people? Louis Antoine de Saint-Just (178), the youngest of the deputies, declared that there need be no trial. Kingship itself was a crime, and the King ought simply to be executed without delay. Robespierre, too, was opposed to a trial. A trial of the King would put the Revolution itself in the dock. But the rest of the Convention accepted the idea, and in December the King was twice brought before them. Standing at the bar (179, *right*), before the seated deputies, Louis denied that he had ever wished to shed the blood of the people. But Louis was quickly to find himself in difficulties. Here he is pictured in prison with his family (180).

During the trial (20th November), secret correspondence was found by Jean-Marie Roland in an iron chest at the Tuileries Palace. These papers revealed that the King had long been playing a double game. But the discussion of the King's guilt was accompanied by great bitterness among the deputies: many of the Brissotins had had an ambiguous attitude to royalty. A hostile caricature shows the royal "menagerie" being driven to the Temple Prison (181). The King is represented by a turkey, the Queen by a wolf-bitch, the King's sister and the royal children by wolf-cubs. The revolutionary driving them says, "They were fattened on our blood and they wished to murder us!"

The end was not far off. Picture (182) is a romantic vision of the King's farewell to his

181

182

family. At about half past ten on the morning of 21st January, 1793, Louis XVI of France was publicly executed. The guillotine was placed in the Place de la Révolution (formerly Place Louis XV, now Place de la Concorde). Surrounded by soldiers and representatives of the forty-eight Paris Sections, Louis made a speech which was drowned by the drums. An illustration of the execution (183), first pub-

lished in 1793, probably shows the victim moments before his death. Soldiers and *sans-culottes* shouted, "Vive le Nation!" when the King's head was held up for all to see (185). Other members of the royal family would soon share a similar fate. Louis's sister, Madame Élisabeth (184), for example, would go to the guillotine herself over a year later on 10th May, 1794.

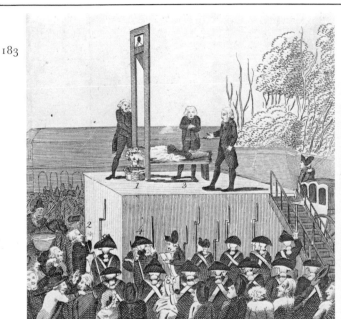

183

184

185

The execution of the King provoked surprisingly little reaction. One reason might have been that, at about this time, the French armies had taken the offensive and had overrun the frontiers both to the northeast and southwest. General Charles Dumouriez routed the Austrians at Jemmappes in November and entered the city of Brussels. The province of Savoy was annexed in the same month. Jemmappes (186) was a great victory for the "nation in arms," and for the democratic army. In face of such victories the royalist *émigrés* were ignored as useless and powerless old men, rather as in a revolutionary cartoon of the time (188). A royalist priest on the right intones empty prayers. The policy of Brissot seemed to triumph (187). "We cannot rest until all Europe is ablaze," he declared. By

186

187

188

the spring of 1793 all the European states, except Scandinavia and Switzerland, were at war with France.

But the French armies were over-extended. The French plundering of Belgium and the anti-clerical policy of the Revolution aroused considerable antagonism from the inhabitants of the battle areas. The Austrians under the Duke of Coburg now attacked, and Dumouriez suffered a reversal of fortunes in the Battle of Neerwinden in March, 1793 (189). Dumouriez was defeated. His solution to this setback was to enter into secret negotiations with Coburg (190). When the Convention in Paris sent representatives to Dumouriez, he at once arrested them. This was an act of open treason. An engraving illustrating the scene is reproduced below (191).

189

191

190

In the meantime, the Convention had other troubles, for the crisis of the Revolution was intensified by the provincial revolt of the Vendée, in Brittany. Initially, this insurrection took place in opposition to the Convention's efforts to impose conscription, to fight the ever-growing patriotic war. The Vendéen insurgents (193) were generally in small groups, and it remained to be seen how effective their cause would be. Religion was an important element in the revolt, as the insurgents (192) fought to preserve something of the old order. The royalist aristocracy were probably taken by surprise by the revolt. But, as a passport given to a released prisoner shows (194), the aristocracy clung to their hopes: the passport claims to be in the first year of the reign of Louis XVII, rather than in the first year of the Revolution.

The defeats and the threat of counter-

192

193

revolution in the west were accompanied by economic distress. The inflation already brought about by the *assignats* was made far worse by the heavy cost of European war. Popular agitation by the *sans-culottes* and "red caps" (196) demanded a remedy for economic distress. The Convention began fully to realize the danger of cutting itself off from the wishes of people. But rather than reduce the war effort, it launched instead a policy of putting on trial all those who were suspected of treason. A Revolutionary Tribunal was set up, to test the "patriotism" of the prisoners. Antoine Fouquier-Tinville (195) was appointed Public Prosecutor. On 6th April, 1793 the Committee of Public Safety (197) assumed the executive power of the French nation. At first, Danton and Barère were the Committee's most important members. The Convention then took steps to increase the war effort.

PASSEPORT.

Nous commandants des armées catholiques & royales avons accordé le présent passeport à *Claude Davah de la ville Balançou departeman de l'orme* de teur a *Chollet* ——————— prisonnier de guerre renvoié, aprés avoir eu les cheveux coupés, audit lieu de *Chollet*.

le —— quel —— à —— promis & juré sur *Son* honneur & serment de ne jamais reprendre & porter les armes contre sa Maiesté trés chrétienne Louis dix-sept, qu'il —— reconnoi —— pour unique & légitime souverain ni contre la religion catholique apostolique & romaine ——————— donné à *Chollet* ———————

——————— ce 22 du mois de *juin* 1793. l'an 1.er du regne de louis XVII.

:P: Bureau

194

195

197

196

When all these arrangements had been made, members of the Convention were sent out to the provinces of France to raise an army of 300,000 men. The war effort was to be increased; there would be no economies for the "nation in arms." Figure (199) shows a special *représentant du peuple* (people's representative) with the army. These representatives took the place formerly occupied by the officer class in the *ancien régime*; even a democratic and republican army needed leadership and organization. Figure (200) shows the departure of the volunteers as depicted by Émile Boutigny.

From that time onwards, events were largely in the hands of (198, *left to right*): the member of the Commune, the gaoler, the *sans-culotte*,

198

199

200

and the drummer whose task was to summon
the section (of his town) together. Nothing,
however, could now take away the power of
the mob. On 2nd June, 1793, a huge crowd of
Parisian extremists surrounded the Convention, demanding absolute equality for citizens,
an end to economic hardship, and the arrest of
certain moderate members, especially the
Girondins. Inside the Assembly, Georges
Couthon (202), who was paralysed, demanded
to be carried to the tribune (201). Once there,
he asked that the people's demands be accepted. The Girondins had no escape and no
appeal from the tribune, and were led off to
prison, anxiously to await what the future
might hold in store (203).

201

202

203

In deference to the *sans-culottes*, great care was taken to enforce absolute equality of citizenship. The Revolution made strange bedfellows. Members of the Order of Saint-Louis and coalmen were once called at the same time to a municipal office (207). Revolutionary committees were set up throughout France to ensure that this equality was maintained. But in the provinces, a movement was growing against Paris. It seemed that, despite every

cry of equality, liberty and fraternity, the citizens of Paris were, in fact, ruling France. In Lyons a Revolutionary Tribunal attacked the Jacobins (205). Its resistance was short-lived—the Tribunal was destroyed in October, 1793, after a two-month siege.

In July, Robespierre joined the Committee of Public Safety. An aura of mystification was encouraged by Danton's withdrawal from affairs, at this time, following the failure of his

204

205

206

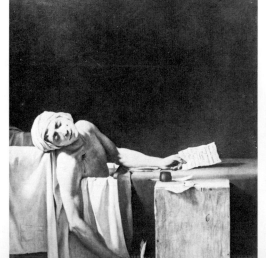

207

recent attempt to negotiate peace with Austria and Prussia. A sense of peril, too, was emphasized when the crippled Marat was assassinated in his bath of mineral salts on 13th July. Jacques-Louis David's great memorial painting of the event hangs at Versailles (206). Marat's assassin was a woman, Charlotte Corday, a political zealot who was at once arrested and guillotined before a large crowd in Paris (204). "I killed one man," she said, "in order to save a hundred thousand."

Feeling that the Revolution was in danger, the representatives of the people tried to inspire the troops with a higher morale. An extravagantly dressed representative asked his fellow troops, "What are you worried about?" (208). A painting by Béricourt depicts what was soon to become a common sight in the streets—the arrest of a citizen on suspicion while a crowd of passers-by looks on (209).

208

209

France had now entered in the fearful period of mass suspicions, trials, and executions which is commonly called "the Terror." No one could feel safe under the shadow of the guillotine, either in Paris or in the provinces. France was in the bloodiest phase of her history.

Picture (210) shows a Revolutionary Tribunal at work. A well-dressed French gentleman, his wife and daughter are escorted into the court room for examination; the members of the Tribunal all wear revolutionary bonnets, and some of them lounge about drinking and smoking. The summary justice of such courts was greatly feared by those thrown on their mercy.

A new figure became familiar at public guillotinings: the *tricoteuses* (212), the implacable women who continued knitting

210

211

silently during the executions. Those who suffered most were the nobility who had not yet fled the frontiers of France, and who were now rounded up and thrown into the gloomy dungeons of the notorious Conciergerie Prison, near the Palace of Justice in Paris (211). Marie-Antoinette herself was executed in October, 1793. David made a famous sketch of the former Queen on her way to the scaffold (213). A rare coloured engraving shows her last moments before the guillotine fell (214). Her cousin, the Duke of Orleans, famed for his intrigues in the early days of the Revolution, was also executed in 1793. When picture (215) was first published, it carried the cynical caption:

"The martyr of equality: behold the progress of our system."

212

214

213

215

In October, 1793, twenty-one deputies of the Gironde were arrested and executed (216). One of their number, Charles Valazé (217), managed to commit suicide first, but the authorities hung his corpse in vengeance just the same. It was actions like this which helped to earn these months the name of "the Terror."

Charles Barbaroux, pictured here leading the march of the Marseillais on Paris three years before (218), was also executed.

Priests were among those most relentlessly persecuted. Legends grew up around those who for one reason or another had escaped. One legend told the story of two priests who

216
217

218

were spared by a miraculous intervention of the Virgin Mary (219).

Gradually, the situation for the Republic began to improve. Jean-Baptiste Drouet (221), the postmaster who had recognized Louis on his flight out of Paris to Varennes, and now a member of the Convention, urged his colleagues to renounce all inhumanity. But when the city of Lyons was recaptured by the revolutionary forces, an extremely savage repression followed, and scenes of horror were recorded (220). Toulon, which had fallen into English hands, was likewise recaptured, in December (222).

219

220

221

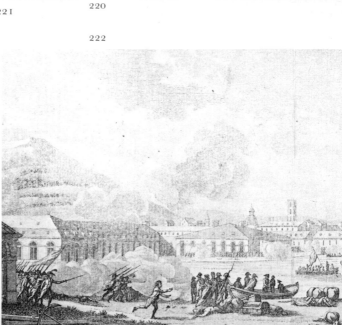

222

93

In November, 1793, the insurgents in the Vendée were forced to move to positions north of the River Loire (223). On the other side, they roamed about in great disorder, and every defeat was followed by the ruthless shooting of hundreds of fugitives. Jean-Baptiste Carrier, who was the representative of the people at Nantes, wrote a black chapter in history, when he had 2,000 people drowned in the River Loire between November, 1793, and January, 1794 (225). He would hear no pleas for mercy (224).

At the same time as carrying out savage repressions, the government sought to celebrate republican virtues. An example is supplied in a number of pseudo-religious parades

223

224
225

226

LE PEUPLE FRANÇAIS
RECONNAIT L'ÊTRE SUPRÊME
ET L'IMMORTALITÉ
DE L'ÂME

which it sponsored (229). In May, 1794, the Convention decreed the existence of the so-called "Supreme Being." The decree insisted that everyone must believe in this being, and not confuse it with the God of the Christian Churches. The main tenet of the new religion was worship of Nature, as illustrated in a "visual aid" used in French schools (226). An engraving (227) shows Robespierre leading a Festival of the Supreme Being through the streets of Paris. Many such festivals were held for the strange new cult. On a famous one, effigies of Atheism, Ambition and Egoism were burned before a statue representing Wisdom. An engraving showing this festival is reproduced below (228).

227

228

229

Among the many people arrested during the Terror was the famous chemist Antoine Lavoisier, who was taken in his laboratory while soldiers searched his equipment (230). It was said that Republican France needed no learned men. Lavoisier was guillotined on 8th May, 1794. The end was also near for Danton. He and his followers were finally arrested and executed on 5th April, 1794. He could no longer seem to support Robespierre's leadership. At his trial, Danton's huge voice and dynamic energy dominated the court room, but it was to no avail (231). One of the last people to fall during the Terror was the young poet André Chénier (232), who was seized for protesting against the bloodbath.

230

He was guillotined at the age of thirty-one, two days before the overthrow of Robespierre.

All this terrible revolution and energy bore some fruit, however, for the armies of France became stronger. Very soon they had driven back the invaders, and by the spring of 1794 they had crossed beyond their own frontiers, and were pushing all before them. The real organizer of victory was Lazare Carnot (233), and the decisive victory was the Battle of Fleurus, fought on 26th June, 1794, under the command of Jean-Baptiste Jourdan. Soon, French soldiers set foot in Antwerp and Brussels. The counter-revolution was in danger. Now that the national emergency was over, did the government still need the Terror?

232

231

233

Robespierre claimed that the Terror was even more necessary than before. He strenuously called for a still tighter grip on government, for more "republican virtue," and for one final purge. He managed to have Collot d'Herbois expelled from the Jacobin Club, because he did not agree (234). Robespierre now had too many opponents. On 27th July (9th Thermidor in the new Revolutionary calendar) he was prevented from speaking at the Convention. That same evening, Robespierre tried to shoot himself, or was shot in the jaw; it is not certain which. Picture (235) gives the latter version. Next day, Robespierre, Saint-Just, Georges Couthon and many others were executed. Robespierre was virtually dead (236) by the time he reached the guillotine. The worst part of the Revolution was over.

234

235

236

CHAPTER FIVE

THE REACTION: FROM DIRECTORY TO BONAPARTISM

THE PERIOD THAT FOLLOWED the death of Robespierre (237) has often been neglected. It is seen either as an anti-climax to the greatest period of the Revolution, or as a prelude to the Bona-partism which has left its own indelible mark on later French history.

The Directory—the new French con-stitution which followed the Terror—always contained the elements of its own destruction. In constitutional terms, the state had a divided executive, and a complicated legislative system; the coun-try stood perpetually on the eve of elections which kept up the appearance rather than the reality of democracy. Such a system was ill-adapted to crisis. It is understandable that statesmen of the Directory should have turned more and more to the army as the one source of real strength. In political terms, all the options still seemed open. Royalists believed that the restoration of the monarchy stood an increasing chance of success. Jacobins felt that a return of crisis and emergency would necessitate a return to the methods and ideals of 1793. France was tremen-dously alive with political ideas.

Economically speaking, the problem was to find a mean between extreme shortage of food and the misery which this caused, and a catastrophic fall in food prices which accompanied superabundant harvests. The currency was unreliable; government finance lacked stability. When faced with discontent, the government had only the weapon of the army.

So, in all these ways, the Directory led to Bonaparte. Morally speaking, too, a striking contrast is seen between the mediocre politicians of the Directory, whose qualities were either those of the technician, or those of the skilful intriguer, and the outstanding ability of the young generals who had distinguished them-selves in war. A corrupt and materialist society seemed to contrast with a magnifi-cent army, exalted with its glorious achievements. Any one of the generals might have led the *coup d'état* which was to end the Directory. But by 1799 Lazare Hoche, François Marceau and Bartholomé Joubert were dead; Jean Moreau lacked the will. It was Bonaparte, combining a romantic vision with an acute political sense, who took the necessary steps.

Such an analysis suggests that the period of the Directory was merely a parenthesis. But it neglects much of the Directory which was valuable. The Directory was an attempt to end the cycle of repressions and risings; it sought to create a system of parliamentary government; it saw and encouraged a movement of intellectual and artistic freedom. The Directory, in certain respects, resembles the France that was to emerge from the Napoleonic Wars. One might imagine a Louis-Philippe, a Napoleon III or an Adolphe Thiers ruling over Directory society. This is to confirm, rather than to deny its repressions, its injustices and its foreign adventures. But it is also to suggest that it stood for something permanent in France. Perhaps it is Bonapartism rather than the Directory which is the parenthesis.

237

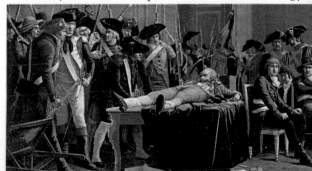

After the fall of Robespierre in 1794, a reaction set in, often known as the "Thermidorian Reaction," after the current date in the Revolutionary calendar. The French felt a nausea after so much killing, and at last the nation retreated from the Terror. A mythology grew up about those who were the last to be guillotined, and painters pictured the "last cart" which rattled to the place of execution (238). A legend also grew up about François Hanriot, the Commander of the National Guard, who was executed at the same time as Robespierre. A drawing by Alfred Johannot shows him insisting that the condemned should be guillotined in the last days of the Terror (240). Antoine Fouquier-Tinville (239) and Jean-Baptiste Carrier were themselves sent to the guillotine, on 8th May, 1795, and

238   239

240

16th December, 1794, respectively. Deputies claimed that they had themselves been secret Girondins, and that they had opposed the Terror. Remembering the blood on their hands, this was a strange charge to make. Many of the men who had helped overthrow Robespierre had been moderates of the Plain. New personalities came forward, many of whom had been silent up to now. One such was Jean Cambacérès (241); a magistrate, he had confined his attentions almost entirely to legal matters. He had voted for the death of Louis XVI only with reservations, and now appeared a partisan of mercy. Jacobinism was dying, although it did not entirely disappear. The Jacobin Club closed (243), and the archetypal Jacobin with *Surveillance!* on his cap and bell in hand (242) went underground.

241

242

243

A characteristic of the new reaction was a general air of relaxation, and a sudden return to pleasure. The relief was felt especially in Paris, which had been at the focus of events. Elaborate fashions, which had quickly died after 1789, returned to favour and could safely be worn without risk of anti-aristocratic prejudice. The end of Jacobin puritanism was succeeded not only by freedom of morals, but an atmosphere of speculation; gambling rooms with their card tables and roulette wheels became very popular (244, 245).

The revolt in the Vendée was now coming to an end. The leader of the insurgent army, Henri La Rochejacquelin, had been killed by a republican soldier on 4th March, 1794. But

244 246

245

already he had been having talks with the republicans. In February, 1795, his successor, Charette de la Contrie, signed the treaty of peace in the outskirts of Nantes. Vendéen military equipment was handed over to the republicans (246), and the various leaders of rebel groups made their submissions. They were granted an amnesty, they had their property returned (or were indemnified), they were excused military service. Freedom of worship was granted even to the non-juring priests. This was important, as it was impossible not to grant the rest of the French people what had been granted only to the rebels. From February, 1795, religious practices were no longer offences against society.

But to attack the memory of Robespierre, to pacify the Vendéens, to cultivate dress and gambling, all this did not resolve the economic problems. The winter and the spring of 1795 were extremely hard. Paper money no longer commanded any confidence. The government had given up control of prices.

On 1st April, 1795 (12th Germinal in the Revolutionary calendar), and 20th May (1st Prairial), the *sans-culottes* of Paris rose in violence for the last time. Women *sans-culottes* (249) became legendary, and in these uprisings women were prominent figures.

An engraving (248) depicts one of the incidents of Germinal. The National Guard prevented Billaud-Varennes, Collot d'Herbois and Barère from leaving Paris, where they had been sentenced to deportation. The insurgents told one another that the Convention was in flight, but they were much mistaken: a full

248

247

249

repression followed. Between 3,000 and 4,000 people were thrown into prison.

In religious matters the worship of the Supreme Being was abandoned. The religion of Theophilanthropy, the worship of the Author of Nature, persisted, but it too declined. Figure (247) shows a ceremony of baptism under the Nature cult. The Goddess of Reason (250) was no longer. By the middle of 1795, the reaction was carried so far that constitu-tional monarchy itself might have been restored. But on 8th June, Louis XVII (251) died in his captivity, and monarchist hopes were dashed. Louis was said to have died of a scrofulous disease, but the monarchists never believed this. They believed either he had been poisoned, or that he was still alive. The Comte de Provence, in Verona, now became Louis XVIII, and declared that he would never compromise with the Revolution.

250

251

The crown continued to reduce its chances by associating itself with foreign intervention and civil war. It helped to persuade Britain to land an expeditionary force of *émigrés* at Quiberon Bay on the French coast. But this force was crushed by the republican armies under General Lazare Hoche, and nearly 750 were killed. The insurgents (*chouans*) were divided among themselves. An engraving (252) shows the surrender at Quiberon on 22nd July, 1795. A cartoon of the same year mocks the *chouans* and other counter-revolutionaries (253).

The Press now underwent a revival, and republican newspapers began to attack the royalists. It was possible to recall the old days of Press freedom as shown in caricatures (255).

A new constitution had to be devised, which would return to something like the system of

252

253

1791, and many moderates feared that a conservative Assembly would be royalist. The Convention therefore decreed that two-thirds of the next legislature should be chosen from its own ranks, meaning in effect that it would be republican. On 5th October, 1795 (13th Vendémiaire), a royalist rising threw Paris into turmoil. Coming together at the Church of Saint-Roch the royalists found themselves under heavy artillery-fire (254). The insurgents numbered between 20,000 and 25,000. The Convention, however, had called in large forces of troops and put them in charge of officers who had been placed on the non-active list. These included the young General Napoleon Bonaparte. Legend has it that Bonaparte was in charge of the artillery (256). In fact, he was not on the spot when the firing took place.

254

255

256

The new constitution came into force. The Directory, indeed, inaugurated a new age in this troubled period. The 750 deputies, elected by an electorate of 30,000 wealthy citizens, were divided into two chambers. The 250 eldest, chosen by lot, took their seats in the Conseil des Anciens (Council of the Elders); the remainder formed the Conseil des Cinq-Cents (Council of Five Hundred). The law insisted that the deputies should wear special costumes, designed by the famous artist Jacques-Louis David (263). The designs were inspired by the traditions of Ancient Rome. An Ancien wore costume resembling a toga (259). The Cinq-Cents (257) wore one of similar design but simpler appearance. The govern-

257

258

259

260

261

262

ment executive was in the hands of the Directors, who also had an elaborate and distinctive dress (258).

Other officers of the government were given special costumes. The Secretaries of the Councils and of the Executive wore distinctive feathered hats (260), and a sober uniform of a rather legal character. Municipal officers (261) had the same kind of breeches, and a coat, with a tricolor sash around their shoulder and waist. The judges, on the other hand (262) dressed more like the Conseils, with a bordered toga, and a Renaissance-style hat. These costumes suggest that France at that time was highly conscious of carrying upon her shoulders the burden of history.

263

The Cinq-Cents drew up a list of fifty names, out of which the Anciens chose the five Directors, these were the officials in charge of five new divisions of government: diplomacy, war, police, administration and the execution of the laws. This division into five would, it was hoped, prevent any recurrence of dictatorial power, as France had suffered before. The most able of those chosen was Paul Barras (266). The candidate who received the greatest number of votes in this election, however, was Ossian La Revellière-Lepeaux (268), a bourgeois from Poitou who by his anti-clericalism and Deism recalled the atmosphere of 1789. Lazare Carnot, Jean Reubell, and Étienne Letourneur were the other Directors. All five were politicians of long-standing, all had voted for the guillotining of Louis XVI.

264
265
266
267

The Directory now had to face two tasks: to solve the economic problem, and to determine foreign policy. There were some who believed that revolutionary France was, by her very nature, bound to have wars with nearby nations. How could a republic live peacefully with monarchies? Cartoons of the time vividly portrayed the threat that the Revolution was felt to pose to the old monarchies. Figure (267) shows a French patriot turning the handle of an electric machine which sends a current through the thrones of Europe. Figure (264) portrays French revolutionaries feeding Europe with the bread of liberty, and (265) the Revolution in the figure of a locust, the age-old emblem of destruction and famine. Figure (269) depicts the brotherhood of peoples, eating richly at the same table.

268

raine donnant aux Despotes renverse leurs Trônes

269

At first it had seemed that the fall of Robespierre meant peace in Europe, as well as the relaxation of the tempo of revolution. But French terms were always hard, and only a partial peace was made with Prussia (April, 1795), Holland (May, 1795) and Spain (July, 1795). An engraving (270) shows crowds in Amsterdam celebrating peace and the signing of the alliance between the French and Batavian republics. Symbols of the *ancien régime* are being joyfully burned. France annexed Dutch Flanders, and was also paid an indemnity. The major powers were forced to accept that France should incorporate Belgium, but the war against Austria and England continued. In September, 1795, French troops crossed the Rhine (271) and advanced on Mainz, but shortly afterwards

270

271

they were forced back from their positions.

Above all it was against the Italians that the Directory went to war. With exaggerated ideas of the wealth of Tuscany and Lombardy, Genoa and Venice, the Directors gave Bonaparte command. The result was a series of resounding victories. The Battle of Mondovi, fought on 22nd April, 1796 (272), was one of six triumphs won in fifteen days.

The taking of the bridge at Lodi on 10th May, 1796, was also celebrated in France, for example on this playing-card (273). This was a great item of the growing Bonapartist propaganda, but although the battle was a French victory, the Austrian army in fact withdrew, and avoided final defeat. After many other conquests, the Peace of Campo-Formio brought a profitable peace, in October, 1797.

272

PRISE DU PONT DE LODI.
défendu par 30 bouches à feu
et 30 000 hom.ˢ Autrichiens
en 1796

273

After his great victories in Italy, celebrated by a great military parade through the streets of Paris (274), Bonaparte next sought his destiny in Egypt. An engraving of the time represented him as a Frenchman from one angle and a turbaned Egyptian from another (275). When Horatio Nelson destroyed the French fleet at Aboukir Bay, however, Bonaparte and his army found themselves in a difficult situation, cut off from their lines of supply. Nelson and the British feared that Bonaparte would even try to strike at India. The Directory, even without Bonaparte, seemed destined to perpetual war everywhere in Europe. The campaigns in Italy continued under new commanders, and on 15th February, 1798, General Louis Berthier's troops triumphantly entered Rome (277).

274

275

276

What were the effects on the Directory of these continued efforts abroad? The economic situation remained a very difficult one. The paper issues of *assignats* (279) were continually losing their value. Soon their real value would hardly equal the cost of printing them. The *rentier* (stockholder) (276) was one class of Frenchman to be badly hit.

On 19th February, 1796, the production of *assignats* was finally ended. There seemed to be no point in going on with them. The printing plates were solemnly and publicly burned in the Place Vendôme in Paris (278). The Directory tried instead to solve its financial problems by a policy of forced loans, issuing unpopular demands on different sections of society. But money came in only after long delays, as everyone sought to evade collection.

277

278

279

The well-being of the country still depended to a great extent on its harvests. The lack of confidence meant that provincial markets were often deserted. In the towns there was hunger; in the countryside vagabondage. There came "The Conspiracy of the Equals," led by François Baboeuf (280). This was a socialist movement, partly utopian in aim and outlook, but partly contemporary in that it vested power in a revolutionary élite. Baboeuf himself was arrested in 1796 and executed for treason in 1797. The Directory proved that it could maintain itself in power through the army. The Directory organized lavish festivals. Among them were the Festival of Victory held in 1796 (281), and the Festival of Science and

280

281

282

283

Art in 1798 (283). The five Directors are seen reviewing art treasures, exotic animals and other trophies looted from other countries. These festivals were intended to fortify the French people during economic and social distress. The Directory style of living was in some respects lavish, and provided the prosperous middle class with a café-society devoted to entertainment. Many prints and engravings survive from this period, for example: (284) a middle-class café; (285) another scene of Directory fashion and entertainment; and (282) an extravagant public firework display. The Montansier Theater was famous for its foyer (286), where daringly dressed women awaited admirers and customers.

284

285   286

Directory society also boasted a considerable number of talented individuals who led French tastes and fashions. Bernardin de Saint-Pierre for example, who taught at the École Normale Supérieure, was something of an echo of the past (287): he remained faithful to the ideas and idealism of Rousseau and to Deism. André Ampère, a scientist, pioneered the use of electricity, and gave his name to a unit of electrical measurement. Madame de Staël the daughter of Necker and one of the leading intellectuals of the time, was committed to the idea of constitutional government (288). She was one of the most controversial members of salon society. Madame Récamier, a friend of Barras, was a famous beauty of the age.

Politically speaking the regime was an improvisation. Since its executive was divided into five branches, it had little authority. Nor was this its only difficulty: because of recent

287

288

289

290

history, it was threatened by many other allegiances—Jacobins, royalists, republicans, moderates. Perhaps it was not only Talleyrand who was uncertain in which direction to turn (289), as a cartoonist suggested (although Talleyrand did gain a reputation for being a man for all seasons). Events began to move rapidly. Bonaparte returned hurriedly from Egypt, though only a few people knew. Then, on 19th November, 1799, a pretext was used to force the Cinq-Cents out of Paris to Saint-Cloud. It was to be the end of the Directory, and the beginning of a new phase. Bonaparte's soldiers took the Cinq-Cents into custody (291). The Directory was replaced by the rule of the Three Consuls—Bonaparte, Jean Cambacérès and Charles Lebrun—commemorated on a medal of 1799 (290). A cartoon by Isaac Cruickshank dismissed Napoleon as a mere toy soldier (292).

291

292

As had happened before during the Revolution, power was falling into the hands of the powerful. The Directory may have achieved much in restoring law and order and humanity into domestic affairs, but it could not really hope to offer a permanent solution to the problem of French government. At the time of Bonaparte's arrival at the forefront of events, it had not been long enough established to command deep loyalties of its own. It could still be prey to a military *coup d'état*, especially if conducted by a general with a success and popularity as great as that of the young Bonaparte. The Consuls, of whom Bonaparte was now one, took possession of the Tuileries (293). A royal government—if of a new kind—

293

was well on its way. Would the Revolution have succeeded or failed?

It has been easy to condemn the Directory. One French historian made a just remark when he said that the Directory represented an attempt to live a normal life in an abnormal situation. This was an experience which many governments of France were to know in later years. The inheritance of the Revolution was a heavy one. There were many interests, many pressure groups, and many ideologies. The administrative system was weak and ineffective, and the Directors themselves were ordinary men, seeking compromise solutions in difficult and complicated circumstances.

Napoleon won victories for France, and had defeated the forces of the European alliance at Arcole in 1796. An engraving shows the crossing of the bridge at Arcole by the French troops, after which victory soon came (296). Baron Antoine de Gros painted Napoleon in his hour of glory (294). Both these pictures depict a romantic view of Napoleon as leader and standard-bearer of his country, and many contemporaries were not surprised at his sudden rise to political as well as military power. A more cynical viewpoint was also current. The Englishman James Gillray, cartooned Napoleon in military uniform driving out the forces of equality from France (295). A contemporary French cartoon de-

294

picted the monster of the French Revolution nurturing its infant, Bonaparte, who would grow in its likeness (297). It remained to be seen whether, in the years to come, these prophecies would be fulfilled.

Napoleon was an unusual man. He had tremendous energy, a remarkable memory, and a quick and agile mind. He was intensely practical, but he could also be a dreamer; he had a perception of his own greatness, but he was often petty and cynical. It is not surprising that he should have so fascinated both his contemporaries and posterity. But it was to the Revolution that he owed his destiny; the greatness of those events had rubbed off on him.

295

EXIT LIBERTÈ a la FRANCOIS! — or — BUONAPARTE closing the Farce of Egalitè at S.t Cloud near Paris Nov.r 10.th 1799.

296

297

PICTURE CREDITS

The Author and Publishers wish to thank the following for permission to reproduce the illustrations in this book: Trustees of the British Museum, 54; French Government Tourist Office, 20–1; the Mansell Collection, 22, 64, 78, 85–6, 89–90, 99, 102, 104, 107, 112, 120, 125, 131, 138–41, 143, 163, 166, 168–70, 172–3, 180–1, 183, 185, 189, 191–2, 194, 200, 203–4, 207, 209, 211, 219–20, 222, 226, 228, 233, 241–3, 247–8, 251, 260–3, 265, 267, 272, 275, 277, 280–1, 283–4 and 288; *Radio Times* Hulton Picture Library, 9, 19, 58, 60, 87, 93, 95, 103, 113, 121–2, 126, 128, 150, 153, 155, 164, 178, 184, 190, 201–2, 212, 215, 231, 234, 239–40, 249, 253, 264, 266 and 269; the Weaver Smith Collection, 4–8, 10–18, 23–6, 51–2, 65, 68–9, 79, 81–2, 91, 145, 154, 156, 167, 171, 186, 193, 196–7, 199, 218, 223–5, 227, 230, 235, 238, 252, 256–9, 271, 292 and 296. Other illustrations in this book are the property of the Wayland Picture Library.

FURTHER READING

For general histories of the French Revolution (in English) the reader should consult:

Alfred Cobban, *A History of Modern France* Vol. 1, 1715–1799 (Penguin Books, 1961, and Jonathan Cape, 1962).
A. Goodwin, *The French Revolution* (Hutchinson, 1953, and Grey Arrow, 1959).
Norman Hampson, *A Social History of the French Revolution* (Routledge, 1963).
Georges Lefebvre, *The French Revolution* 2 volumes (translated; Routledge, 1962 and 1964).
George Rudé, *Revolutionary Europe* (Collins, Fontana, 1964).
M. J. Sydenham, *The French Revolution* (Batsford, 1965).

Other books, dealing with particular aspects and which can be recommended are:

P. Amann, *The Eighteenth Century Revolution: French or Western?* (D. C. Heath, 1963).
C. B. A. Behrens, *The Ancien Régime* (Thames and Hudson, 1967).
Richard Cobb, *A Second Identity* (Oxford, 1969). This is a collection of essays, many of them concerned with the French Revolution. The same author's article on the revolutionary mentality in *History* (1957) is strongly recommended.
Alfred Cobban, *The Social Interpretation of the French Revolution* (Cambridge, 1964).
Aspects of the French Revolution (Jonathan Cape, 1968). A collection of essays.
D. M. Greer, *The Incidence of the Terror during the French Revolution* (Cambridge, Mass., 1935).
J. Kaplow, *Elbeuf During the Revolutionary Period* (Baltimore, 1964).
G. Lefebvre, *The Coming of the French Revolution* (translated; Princeton, 1957).
The Thermidorians (translated; Routledge, 1965).
The Directory (translated; Routledge, 1965).
Joan McDonald, *Rousseau and the French Revolution* (Athlone Press, 1965).
G. Rudé, *The Crowd in the French Revolution* (Oxford, 1959).
Interpretations of the French Revolution (Historical Association Pamphlet, G.47, 1961).
M. J. Sydenham, *The Girondins* (Athlone Press, 1961).
Albert Soboul, *The Parisian Sans-culottes and the French Revolution* (translated and abridged; Oxford, 1964).
J. M. Thompson, *Robespierre and the French Revolution* (Teach Yourself History Series 1952).
Charles Tilly, *The Vendée* (Edward Arnold, 1964).